AF881303

The Secret Place

The Secret Place

by L.W. Stevenson

Ill. by Kaye Pomaranc

Copyright ©1981 by L.W. Stevenson

Academy Chicago
360 N. Michigan Ave.
Chicago, Illinois 60601

Library of Congress Cataloging in Publication Data

Stevenson, L. W. (Leland W.), 1916-
The secret place.

1. Nature. I. Title.
QH81.S8595 574 81-3495
AACR2

Worlds

WE ARE NOT the only world moving through time and space: there are worlds within worlds. Each seems independent, yet each is awesomely dependent on the others.

There is the microscopic world of a drop of pond water. The hawk flies in another world. The ant hill is yet another.

But the most exciting worlds are those which exist in the human mind. They are the only ones with no set pattern. They are places of self-created sunshine and shadows. Everyday objects and events are recycled into dreams and fantasies as real as any set pattern, although these worlds are as far removed from reality as the star from the bee.

The best of all worlds is created when reality is joined to make believe. We are most adept at this when we are very young.

Reality grows stronger as we grow older.

However, time and reality never win total victory. Once in a great while, we remember and we return to that wonderful place we once knew.

We are often allowed to return to that place of self created wonders with a companion. Our guide is a child. We go back to the world of make believe with a small boy or girl and see it again, through the eyes of a child.

A grandchild is a very special guide, for parents may be so concerned with showing a child how it is to live in the real world that the world of make believe is overlooked. Parents spend a great deal of time running obstacle courses that grandparents have already run.

Grandparents are permitted to remember and to understand and to share and, most precious of all, they are gifted with the grandchild's sharing.

This is the story of a grandson, Steven, and a grandfather, Steve, who shared a world. It is a journal of fourteen years of world-sharing in a very special place. It is, unabashedly, a book of memories.

Thank you, Steven, for sharing the magic of childhood wonder.

Thank you for sharing the Secret Place.

We Name The Secret Place

IF A PLACE is lived in and greatly loved, it should have a name. It is even more important that a place should have a name when it is shared with another person; mentioning that name will call up shared memories.

We call our world the Secret Place. We call it that because it is our world and we share it only with those who deserve the sharing. It has been called the Secret Place since Steven was very young.

Few people visit the Secret Place. It is removed from travelled ways and the occasional hunter or fisherman who passes through will not see the part that is ours. Remember, we created that part.

The name was settled on one Sunday afternoon as Steven and I were returning from a river hike.

Our house in the real world sits beside a much travelled country road. Cars and trucks and huge farm vehicles pass along this road, north and south. Our Amish Dutch neighbors, the plain people, wave to us from their horse-drawn buggies and wagons.

The road crosses the river bridge one mile to the south of our house and touches the west edge of the village of Cooks Mills. We have a Baptist Church to worship in and a general store to visit in and houses with good friends and neighbors.

When the land around us was swamp and prairie grass and the wolves still howled at night, a man named Cook owned a mill on the river. He ground grain and made flour and corn meal for the other settlers. Mr. Cook has been dead many years and no trace remains of his mill but the village still bears his name.

Legend tells that surveyors hammered the barrel of a musket into the ground as a starting place for their measurements. At one time the settlement could boast of a brick kiln, post office, barber shop and other places of business but the railroad was built a few miles east and the village never grew.

A few hundred yards east of our house, the world of general stores and churches and cars and farm machinery no longer exists. It is the world of the Secret Place.

We hike down a lane with the corn field to our left and the forest to our right. We pass the shallow pool where the family of frogs once lived. We pause to study a thicket of poke berry bushes and thorn trees. The underbrush is a tangle of living and dead blackberry bushes. In season, there are wild strawberries. There may be a rabbit or some quail in that tangle for this is one of the favored stopping places of the wild things. A drainage ditch passes the edge of the thicket and is tiled under the lane to wind its way to the pond at the south edge of the forest.

We reach the end of the lane and stand a moment beside the huge, squared corner post. This post marks the beginning of the hill. Sizable hills are an uncommon sight in this flat farm land but this one slopes gently for a respectable distance and ends in the flats of the river bottoms. We once saw five intertwined snakes sunning themselves on a bare spot of ground next to the corner post.

We stand a moment and savor the view of the hill, the river and the trees.

To the north we see the sassafras trees and the grove of maple and oak where we once saw a huge bird soar from a dead tree limb. Barely visible through those trees, we see the silo tops and barn roofs of our Amish neighbors.

At our right hand is the horse pasture of another Amish neighbor and, at the end of that pasture, rows of beehives.

Looking east toward the river we see the grove of maples where we built the Indian hogan. The grove marks the high water line of the river and some of the lower tree limbs are draped with dried weeds and river debris. They look as though they are decorated with poorly put together leis.

We can see the cottonwood tree. It towers over its lesser neighbors and wears its paler colors in all seasons. It is different. It stands out because it is different. We wonder how it arrived in this alien land of shorter trees and darker colors. We think it may not be so important in the plan that it is of different height and color for it has survived and it is there.

The cottonwood is the first familiar sight as we top the hill, going to the river and the last as we return home. To this day we observe the ritual of pausing at the top of the hill as though we are saying, "Hello," or, "Good-bye," to the cottonwood.

Now we walk past the old abandoned tractor sheltered by three walnut trees and arrive at the clump of weeds where we found the skeleton of a dog. We placed its head and jawbones on the end of a three foot stick and stuck the sharp end of the stick in the ground, in the manner of ancient man's warning of territorial boundaries. It remained there as a warning for several months.

We step over a low slung, two-strand barbed wire fence and we are there. It is the Secret Place.

On the Sunday we named the place, Steven was still so young that he had to be carried the last few hundred yards when we returned home, and I was young enough to be able to backpack him with ease.

It was a time when the weathered old stump, laying half buried in the pasture, was a dragon that must be conquered with a sword whittled from a wooden slat.

We reluctantly started home on that late afternoon. The dragon had been subdued and the vines swung on. The sapling trees had been shinnied up and down and it was time for a glass of chocolate milk.

As we paused at the top of the hill and said goodbye to the cottonwood, Steven stood and stared for a long while.

"Grandpa," he said, "does anyone else know about this place?"

"Steven," I said, "the truth is, other people do pass here once in a great while but they don't see what we see or hear what we hear."

"Why not?"

"Because most people are so concerned with watching where they are going or looking back to where they have been, they can't see the beauty of where they are."

"Good," he said, "this is our very own place. No one else will ever know about it and we will call it the Secret Place."

And that is how our world was named.

OUR SECRET PLACE is not overly impressive, if measured in acres or miles. The western boundary is barely one-half mile from our house. This is where we visit the old cemetery, which we consider part of the Secret Place.

There is no path or road leading to the hilltop where old markers record the life span of a small number of early settlers. The place is reached by climbing a woven wire fence and following one of several cowpaths worn into the meadow ground. The paths wind around briar patches, cross a ditch and ascend a small hill to the quiet place. Passersby on the road near the fence would never suspect the location of this part of our Secret Place.

Once we were hiking down one of the paths to the cemetery to reread the dates and speculate on the life lived between those dates. Most of those lying there died so very young.

As we were walking, Steven slightly ahead, he stopped and extended his hand back toward me, palm down. I waited for him to whisper the reason for stopping. I knew he was observing something, possibly one of the wild things. If so, even a slight movement would mar the happening.

Then I too saw what was meeting us in the path. It was a rabbit, but, for a wild thing, it was completely unaware of its surroundings or of any danger. We watched, fascinated, as it slowly hopped toward us.

It was no more than five feet from us when it came to its senses and realized it was not alone. It leaped into the air, twisted its body in mid-leap, landed, scrambling frantically, and vanished into a briar patch.

We wondered if anyone else had ever met an absent-minded rabbit. We also wondered if it would survive the hunting season. Centuries of inbred survival had momentarily lapsed, a lapse that would have allowed it to meet death on that path.

We hiked on across the meadow, jumped the little stream and walked toward the evergreen trees standing among the unkempt mounds. An evergreen or pine never appears lonely or forlorn except when it is part of a graveyard. All old cemeteries are planted with evergreens, no doubt as a symbol of immortality. Those who have lain here since long before Mr. Cook built his mill, longed for that promised beginning that comes with the end just as we do who stand by their graveside.

On one of our trips to the old cemetery Steven found a cow's skull. The discovery of the skull of a long dead cow may not be an exciting find to a world drummed at by super spectaculars, but to a small boy exploring an old cemetery, it is an event full of questions without answers. Did some wild thing drag the skull from its hiding place, worry it a while in mock combat, then go on to more exciting games? Did the recent rains wash the skull to the top of the ground? We had been on this path many times. Why had we not seen the skull on one of those previous trips?

Suppose, just suppose, we said, we had discovered a human skull?

"What would you do, Grandpa?"

"About what?"

"If we had found a human skull."

"I would probably call the police."

"Would they come out and investigate?"

"No doubt."

"Then that would be the end of the Secret Place. There would be people digging and asking questions and taking pictures."

"What would you do, Steven?"

"I would ask his forgiveness and then I would bury his skull so deep it would never be found again."

I told Steven I liked his plan better than mine.

The river is one half mile east of our house. It is the boundary of the Secret Place when we explore it in that direction. Our river is called the Okaw and it changes its appearance more frequently and more radically than any other place we visit on our hikes.

Midsummer, when the grasses are browned and the river bank creviced with dried mud, we can wade across the Okaw in some places. During the rainy seasons it may be many yards wide and many feet deep. In some months it is a tranquil stream hardly deserving to be called a river. In others it becomes a raging torrent, destroying the river bottom crops and driving the wild things from their burrows and homes.

Our river is fed by rock-strewn, clay gullies and by drainage tiles buried beneath the black soil of the farm lands. The river is often fed clay and top soil along with the water and the currents are heavy and brown. Fishermen think of big, ugly carp and yellow bellied catfish. At other times the waters are clear and clean, almost blue, and it is time for striped bass and drumfish.

The river presents its most striking appearance in the winter, often flooding to many times its normal width. The waters lap up to the blackberry patch on the side of the hill and freeze in motion. The thaw comes and the river slowly retreats to its bed and we listen to the loud popping and cracking as the thin ice loses the support of the water. The retreating flood has left circlets of blue-tinged ice clinging to the tree trunks, looking like little ballet skirts on over-sized hickory and oaks. We tell each other the eerie crackling noises are such sounds as Big Foot would make if he were crashing through the underbrush toward where we are standing. A sight or sound can be anything we wish in the Secret Place.

It is great sport to poke at the frozen edges of the ice with our staffs, adding that sound to the creaking and cracking of the ice.

It was the changing face of the river that made me first realize how much the Place meant to Steven.

There is a place within the Place that became a favorite stopping off play ground on our journeys. Here there is a sharp bend in the course of the river. The waters roll west for a few hundred feet, then veer sharply to the southwest. A sand bar sticks out from the north like a soft, pointing finger. Quickly, the path of the current changes directions again, this time going due west. A few feet from the finger, sand has been deposited through the years and a fine swimming hole has been carved. Floating tree limbs and logs momentarily snag on the jutting sand bar, then tear themselves loose to float further downstream.

There is a long stretch of river, west of the sand bar and the swimming hole, where the current moves more quietly. The river is deeper there and much wider. The willows grow thick along the bank, securing a foothold in the soft edge that no flood has been able to loosen.

Tall trees wear long vines dropping from lower limbs, making sturdy swings. One vine in particular had attached itself to a towering oak. It was possible to hang onto this vine and, with a running start, catapult out over the mud bank and rise above the river itself.

We added a touch of danger by populating the water with crocodiles and piranha fish.

A twenty foot tree trunk had jammed itself into the fork of a living forest giant in some long ago flood and stood leaning like a ladder. There was a spectacular view of that part of the Secret Place if one dared climb the leaning trunk past the crotch of the supporting tree. It was a much loved place.

Then the rains came. It rained for days. The gullies and tiles poured forth a never ending stream of water and top soil. We stood dejectedly half way down the slope of the hill and watched the current tearing at the debris-festooned barbed wire fence. It surged into the blackberry patch and even invaded the crabapple trees. We had never seen such a flood and were concerned about the wild things whose homes had been ravaged.

It was two weeks before we could mud through to our favorite spot and when we reached it we could only stare in disbelief.

Our leaning tree trunk was no longer there. There was no familiar drift at the sandbar and even the sandbar itself had changed shape. The vine had been ripped from the oak by some floating log jam and carried off down stream.

Steven watched the swirling waters wash the newly exposed tree roots clutching at the banks.

"Grandpa," he said, "it's all gone."

"No, Steven," I told him, "it's just changed. Our river changed it. That's what it is supposed to do. The river has been changing this part of the world for years."

"You might as well kill a kid as take away his Secret Place."

Young as he was, he knew that grownups sometimes don't understand and he looked at me to see if I was laughing.

I wasn't laughing; I have lost Secret Places too. We all lose Secret Places. We usually lose Secret Places to age and reality, not to rivers.

"Steven," I said, "we are lucky it was only the river that changed our Secret Place."

We found that Secret Places can be moved and recreated quite easily. If one is changed, the mind helps build another.

We discovered a stopping-off place a few hundred yards up the river. A huge tree lay atop a large pile of drift wood. It had anchored itself far up on the bank; it was so tall that its top branches lay half way across the river's surface.

We would sit on that stranded giant and observe river happenings. We have seen more happenings, more fish leaping, more foraging birds and wild things there than at any other observation point in the Secret Place.

We take our knives and remove bark from the body of the fallen tree, dig a few inches and uncover colonies of strange looking insects. The colonies are intricate networks of tunnels and rooms. As the city is exposed to the light, the citizens rush to nowhere in frantic activity. There is no apparent organized plan of action or escape. The security of such cities has depended on three inches of rotting wood since the colony was founded and evolution saw no need to equip it with any other defense mechanism. Some of the bugs seize tiny eggs and bits of food and crawl through cracks in the trunk or under patches of bark we have left. A new city is on the way and the pattern begins again.

There is a leaning tree at this place, also, and to this

day we observe the ritual of climbing the leaning tree on each trip to the Secret Place.

We located the perfect spot for building our fires. It was a flat parcel of cleared ground, sheltered by a triangle of half grown trees.

Steven discovered the butt of a tree that had been sawed somewhere up stream and had floated to our Place in a time of flood. It had almost the shape of a large rustic seat and it was big enough to accommodate both of us when we felt like sitting and staring into the fire. Steven spent a great deal of time pulling and tugging at the big sawed stump to get it into the right position. When we fished in the deep hole at the west edge of the log jam, we could sit in our rustic chair and watch our bobbers.

This place is decorated in proper season with wild daisies, violets, Queen Anne's lace and a host of other wild flowers we know by their beauty, if not by their names.

We call this place our campsite and it has served us well for many years. When we hike separately, we know without saying that we will meet at the campsite. It is a grand place with more of everything than the first site.

But we have never forgotten our first Secret Place with its vine and leaning tree. We smile as we pass it, each knowing the memories of the other.

Steven doesn't know how clearly I see a small boy swinging out over the river. His knuckles whiten as he grasps the rough vine and he screams in mock fright. His hair flies back from his reddened face.

And Grandpa still stands at the river's edge, proudly counting the number of swings.

THE POND, ANOTHER favored place for observing, lies a few hundred yards south of the squared gatepost at the top of the hill. We visit the pond by walking down the lane that passes the west edge of the Amishman's horse pasture and his beehives and his stormcellar dug for storing eggs and produce. Or we can arrive at the pond by hiking through the woods.

The woods are bordered by a barbed wire fence that must be climbed, and before we reach the pond we must cross a fallen tree bridge across a side ditch. We must be alert for poison ivy and poison oak and there are briar patches and thorn trees that clutch at our shirts and our pant legs.

However, the woods are home for land terrapins, snakes, rabbits, squirrels, deer and an occasional fox.

This is where I cut my winter's supply of fireplace logs, thanks to the neighbor who owns the forest. Since each tree seems irreplaceable to Steven, I explain that we fell only selected trees and that the hickory, maple and oak we leave standing may reach for the sunlight without crowding and so grow straighter and taller.

The pond is approximately one-half acre in size and is contained at the deep south end by an earth and rock dam. A draining tile comes from the field across the road and feeds the pond at its more shallow north end. Turtles sun themselves on fallen trees lying in the south shallows and the pond is stocked with bass and hybrid blue gill. There are many bullfrogs of varying ages and sizes singing at the water's edge day and night.

One lone, weather-whitened, dead tree stands at the shallow end. The weeds are kept well cropped by a flock of sheep that live in the meadow surrounding the pond.

Steven and I have often sat for long moments on a log near the pond, each trying to outdo the other in silence and immobility.

After a while, the happenings begin. A frog squeaks its high pitched squeal of fright and splashes into the water. A turtle's sharp-nosed head pops up in the middle of the pond and it studies the mossy bank for a few seconds, then sinks back under the surface. One head re-emerges a few feet south and is joined by another and then another. Presently there are a half dozen turtles silently treading water and staring somberly at the bank.

A woodpecker drums a message with its bill on a limb of the lone old tree. It may be sounding a territorial warning or a mating call; perhaps it is just following woodpecker routine. Suddenly, it ceases drumming and intently studies the branch as though trying to memorize the graining pattern of the wood. It sounds a few more rhythmic beats and flies away to audition another tree.

The sun warms the water and a few more turtles go about their business. A snake streaks across the pond at the south end, leaving a miniature wake. Snakes are always in a hurry on land or in the water. They live a furtive, fearful existence. They have never been able to live down their bad public image and they are totally unaware of the fear they inspire. This one reaches the east bank and disappears into the weeds.

The wild things ignore the two eavesdroppers. Then one of us moves and the spell is broken.

Once, after a rain shower, we started home through the woods and decided to check the shallow pools of water captured in the forest floor's sunken spots. We were looking for tadpoles. One weekend we had scooped a dozen of the wrigglers into a glass jar and took them home and turned them loose in a cast iron boiler. In a few days we discovered we had fathered a large family of tiny frogs which we took back to the woods and released under the trees. We were not prepared to face the responsibility of feeding a dozen baby frogs.

We often find terrapins in the woods. They are not the small kind that may be purchased at dime stores but these are wash-pan sized; their shells are a deep rich brown, shading into lighter brown and flecked with gold and yellow. We have the feeling these big, slow moving creatures are unafraid of anything and pull their head and feet back into their shells only because it is the terrapin way of doing things.

One Saturday morning we carried a large specimen home and placed it on our porch. Whichever direction we pointed its head, it seemed to favor travelling in that direction and set off with much scrambling and scratching on the porch floor. It didn't seem to care what it was doing or which way it was going just so it was doing something and going somewhere. This is not such poor philosophy for a terrapin, for they move so slowly that they must persist.

We carved Steven's initials and the day's date on its back and carried it back across the road and placed it gently beside the bush where we had found it. There was no scrambling and scratching this time. It had tired of our games and was going to wait us out. We left it by its bush and walked on to the pond and when we returned, the terrapin had departed and taken its shell with its date and initials, and found another hiding place.

We are told terrapins live a long life. We talked of the changed world this one might be carried into if at some future date it was discovered by some other small boy who would take it home to marvel at the date and the initials.

Another Saturday morning, Steven crossed the patio and walked under the apple tree at the corner of our house. I saw him stop and pick something from the ground and look at it for a long while. He cupped his hands around his find and, handling it very carefully, brought it to where I was sitting.

"Grandpa," he said, "did you ever see anything so beautiful in all your life?"

He held a fat, ugly toad. There are many of them in our yard and they seem unafraid of our closeness. They move in their slow progress from one place to another. They obviously have a destination in mind although one spot of ground would not seem more attractive than another. There must be a reason or promise of some importance else they would not endure so slow and tortuous a method of travel.

This one was snuggled in the boy's hands. It was wrinkled and bumpy and a muddy gray color and altogether uncomely.

"Grandpa," Steven said, "look into its eyes."

I looked into the toad's eyes and saw rare beauty. The eyes were large and soft and a rich brown color, speckled with gold. They were placid and untroubled, not like the wild, darting eyes of a snared bird or trapped animal. Don't doubt until you have looked into the eyes of a toad.

"Grandpa, tell me what it is thinking."

Perhaps it was thinking "If this is it, this is it. I was here, looking as I do now, long before you came out of your cave. I haven't changed but you have grown weaker and more cruel to the things around you. This may be the end for me but my kind has survived all things and we will continue to survive. Can you say this for your kind?"

We placed the toad back on the ground and it resumed its slow, bumpy journey as though nothing had happened.

Somehow, it didn't seem as ugly and awkward as before.

Snakes and Mother Love

NOT ALL MEMBERS of our family are convinced that snakes are a necessary and beautiful part of our world. We have explained that snakes consume an incredible number of bugs and other bothersome things, along with an occasional frog or fish. Snakes, like most wild things, kill only when they are hungry.

Snakes we meet in the Secret Place are fearful of our presence and they, like all other creatures, obey the two great laws of survival. . .run and hide. Sometimes we see only a movement of grasses or hear the rustle of leaves which tell us that once again a snake has proven how frightened it really is. They are unfairly maligned.

We never feel the kinship with snakes we feel for the other wild things we observe; but, we reason, they are there and they must be there for a purpose.

We have seen snakes that have recently gorged themselves on a frog or toad. The snake lies with its body grotesquely distended by the bulk of its victim. It is in such a well fed stupor that it makes no attempt to escape as we gently prod it with our staffs. We wish it were possible to explain to the snake that not all humans are as tolerant of well-fed snakes as we. This one would make an easy target, lying there with its extended belly. We pick it up with our staffs and place it in the shelter of a clump of weeds.

Of all the snakes we have encountered only one has shown resentment at our trespassing on its territory. Steven met it on the hillside a few feet west of the old tractor. Unlike the others, this one stood its ground, bobbing and weaving like a cobra. Its head was flattened and it struck at the end of Steven's staff. It was the snake's hillside, not ours, and it was defending its territory. Later we were told it was probably a spreading adder. Even though its kind is a danger to man, there is no doubt man is a danger to its kind.

What is counted as righteous bravery in one species may be termed as vicious behavior in another. A human defending his territory is an object of admiration, but a snake performing the same deed is regarded with loathing.

We would never imagine a snake showing affection or any of the nobler qualities claimed by man. Snakes have had such poor publicity since the beginning of all snakes that it is difficult to believe so cold-blooded a creature could display emotion.

one would make an easy target, lying there with its extended belly. We pick it up with our staffs and place it in the shelter of a clump of weeds.

Of all the snakes we have encountered only one has shown resentment at our trespassing on its territory. Steven met it on the hillside a few feet west of the old tractor. Unlike the others, this one stood its ground, bobbing and weaving like a cobra. Its head was flattened and it struck at the end of Steven's staff. It was the snake's hillside, not ours, and it was defending its territory. Later we were told it was probably a spreading adder. Even though its kind is a danger to man, there is no doubt man is a danger to its kind.

What is counted as righteous bravery in one species may be termed as vicious behavior in another. A human defending his territory is an object of admieration, but a snake performing the same deed is regarded with loathing.

We would never imagine a snake showing affection or any of the nobler qualities claimed by man. Snakes have had such poor publicity since the beginning of all snakes that it is difficult to believe so cold-blooded a creature could display emotion.

However, we saw a happening that made us appreciate their emotions.

We often meet Mrs. Green as we pass her home on our way to the river. She lives in the weeds that clutter the ditch winding by the woods. She is the most brilliantly green snake we have ever met so it is only natural that we call her Mrs. Green. We see her so frequently that we are concerned if she is not lying in the weeds as we pass. Perhaps another human carrying a staff has passed her home.

One Sunday afternoon we saw her lying by the corner post at the edge of the horse pasture. Her bright green coils shone against the dried grass.

Mrs. Green was not alone. There were five little

snakes intertwined near by. We watched, entranced, as they warmed themselves in the sunlight.

Suddenly Mrs. Green warned her little brood that the enemy of all snakes, large and small, was close by. One by one the little ones slid into an almost invisible crack in the ground near the corner post. After all five baby snakes were safely underground, Mrs. Green vanished into the same hole.

Mother love in a snake? It's nice to think about.

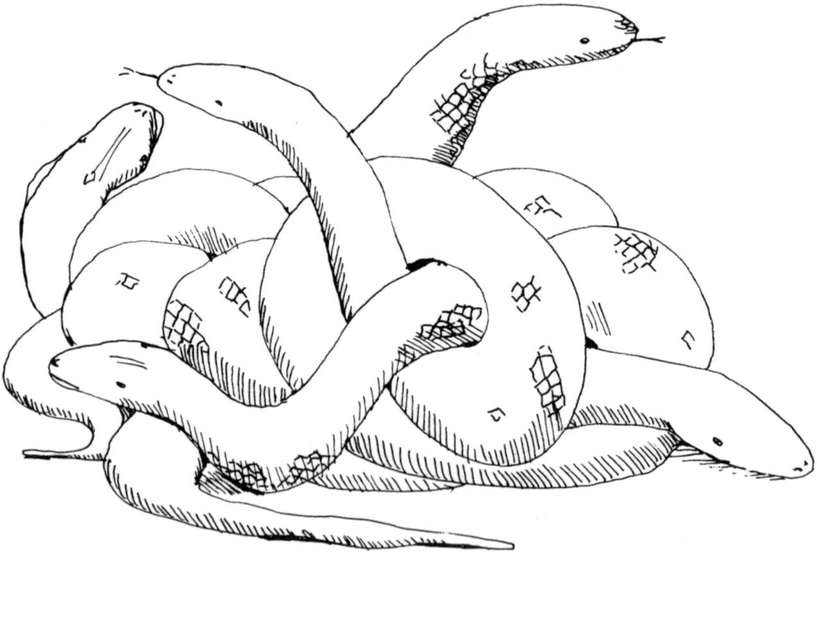

WE NORMALLY SPEND at least a half day on each journey into the Secret Place. The area we explore may not be great in size but there are happenings to observe and time must be spent in conversation and thought.

Day or night, we build campfires. Wood must be gathered and laid by. We search for dry twigs for starting our fires and larger limbs to pile on after the twigs are blazing.

After conversation has ebbed and the fire is dying to red embers, we must dispose of the coals. This is no easy chore if we want to be certain we do not accidentally start a woods fire. There are various ways to extinguish the glowing ashes. Sometimes Steven will scoop water from the river with a coffee can we have cached in a tree fork for that purpose. When the bank is muddy and it is difficult to reach the river, we use the can to scrape dirt from around the campsite and use this to smother the fire. After plastering the firebrands with dirt, we stamp on the ashes with our boots.

At times, we take the smouldering chunks of wood and heave them into the river. Great clouds of steam rise over the water and there is a grand sizzling sound—the stuff of great sea battles. At night the glowing firebrands float downstream into the darkness, giving the appearance of river steamboats with deck lights all ashine.

According to us, we are not cluttering the river. The charred logs float into previously formed drifts and help create fish havens.

Perhaps night fires are the most interesting. We poke at the blazing logs to make sparks spiral upward into the dark leaf canopies. We take turns walking away from the fire into the shadows. We see how closely one can approach the light of the fire without being seen by the other.

We answer the owls hooting around us. We listen to the village dogs talking to their country neighbors. We attempt to interpret the night sounds.

Our night fires normally are of a size that will not alarm the wild things or the neighboring farmers.

Fires are always cause for concern during dry times: a small blaze may feed on a mild breeze until it grows to destroy crops and erase the profits of a year's labor. Dried leaves in the forest may smoulder for an unbelievably long time and then, fanned by a passing wind, race through the underbrush, devastating nests and hiding places. Burning stumps glow for days, sporadically bursting into blue and white flames, then dying to a red glare.

The Secret Place may be savored not only for its beauty and form and the sounds of the woods and the river but for the multitude of odors connected with our journeys. To this day, I cannot visit a floral shop that the displays do not remind me of the meadow and the woods and the variety of blossoms offered by the Secret Place. Unlike humans and animals, no one individual of a flower or plant species may be termed ugly. The three-leafed poison ivy vine possesses a fragile beauty, in spite of its bad reputation. Most wild flowers do not force their sweet smells on one as do domesticated plants. The sweet smell is there but it is more subtle. The river, the wild flowers, the meadow, fresh mown hay, wheat stubble, even the air in the Secret Place must be enjoyed at the proper pace, slowly. People in a hurry miss much.

The smell of burning wood and leaves is one of our favorite memories of the Secret Place. A campfire announces its presence through the thick woods and along the river bank long before the blaze itself is visible.

We build small fires, carefully arranging the wood so no burning embers will ignite leaf fires to spread through the floor of the forest. We leave the fire and explore the river bank and, as we return, the wood smell reaches us long before we sight the big white tree where the baby birds died from hunger.

We use arm-sized logs so they may be more easily extinguished by being tossed into the river. We are very cautious and our fires had never caused us concern until one memorable night.

As we neared the campsite that night, Steven salvaged a big truck tire from a pile of debris left in some floodtime and rolled the tire to the triangle of trees where we build our fires. It was no small chore to move the tire; it was heavily caked with mud and the insides had collected river water that had to be emptied.

We dropped the huge tire on our flame and sat back to watch the blaze and to talk and listen to the river sounds. We immediately discovered we were to watch a very large blaze indeed. We had not known how efficiently a tire burns, nor the amount of heat it would create.

Our fire lighted up the woods and the river banks around our campfire for many feet and the flames leaped high into the air to blacken the leaves of our triangle of trees. The rubber sizzled and popped and the mud baked and the thick, black smoke spiralled into the night.

We became alarmed and dropped to our knees and began scratching leaves and twigs away from the fire bed but the intensity of the heat scorched our already reddened faces and forced us to retreat farther back under the trees.

We ran back and forth to the river with our one coffee can, throwing water from a distance but the puny amounts did little to extinguish the blaze and seemed to cause even more acrid smoke to roll through the woods.

The wild things witnessed the spectacle of two humans down on their knees, frantically scratching at the ground with their bare hands and flailing away at the flames with leafy boughs.

There was a dry meadow on each side of the river and, beyond the meadows, fields of dry corn and soy beans.

We could almost see the alarmed farmers looking out their windows at the big blaze along the river and we expected a caravan of trucks to arrive at any moment.

No truckloads of farmers came to check on us but we did hear the bushes rustle and the twigs pop as though someone were moving toward us from the shadows. We did not know whether they would offer help or give us their opinion of our intelligence.

Once, I stepped to the edge of the shadows and called out that there was really no cause for alarm and that our fire would soon die down. I felt foolish standing there shouting into the darkness under the trees and no one answered so I went back to help with our fire.

At long last, the mud and water shrank our bonfire to a respectable size.

We continued to hear bush-rustling and twig-snapping in the darkness so I walked back under the trees to reassure any irate farmer who might be standing there.

I discovered that our bush rustler was a big gray possum. Its little eyes shone red in the fire light and its pointed nose stuck skyward as it studied the fire and the night and me.

We looked at each other for a few moments; then the possum turned its back on me and slowly walked away, back to bed, I presume. I could almost see it shake its head in disbelief as it left.

We hovered around that oversized fire bed for a long while, pouring water and stomping mud. We arrived home quite late and we never again fueled our fires with a tire.

The Great Hike

IT CAN BE seen that both day and night hiking consume a great deal of time, if done properly.

Sometimes we would plan to take a much longer hike than usual.

We had our route mapped. We would begin at the site of the first Secret Place and follow the course of the river until we arrived at Cooks Mills and the river bridge.

We knew the distance to the bridge to be greater and the adventures more exciting by way of the river rather than the travelled road, and we talked of the thrill of tramping that extra distance, observing new territory and taking notes. We were certain to discover new fishing holes, log jams and boat landing places.

The waters will slash into a field here, undermine a bank further down and form a sandbar at still another place. At times the flow will carve the river into "fish hook" or "S" shapes, doubling back on itself several times in a short distance. The banks rise in steep bluffs at some places along the waterway while in other areas the containing shores are low lying and often flooded. In flood times, carp swim in the inundated corn fields and pastures. There are grassy plots that would serve as lawns for any estate but there are also head-high weeds that must be waded through.

We knew that if we were to make this great hike we must set a definite date and be firm with ourselves in keeping that date. We chose a Saturday and planned an early morning departure.

That Friday night we selected our gear with all the care that might go into outfitting a safari. We stocked my old Army pack with sandwiches and cookies and a soft drink apiece. We packed a notebook for observations and for log-keeping. Perhaps there would be time for a quick sketch of some of the new sights and places.

We slept later into our big day than we had planned and it was almost ten in the morning before we struck out down the lane, walking briskly on the long march. Such a late start seemed an unlikely beginning, but few explorations are without occasional error. We left word at home not to worry: we would probably reach the bridge in the fore part of the afternoon and we had ample provisions.

We lingered awhile at the river bend where the willows grow. It was a beautiful day. The fish were jumping and a muskrat busied itself around some half exposed tree roots near the bank.

We left familiar territory in fifteen minutes and had crossed the base of the bluffs back of the Amishman's house and over into the flat lands before we decided on a break. We were walking beside a dredge ditch we had never seen before and had walked past a boat landing we had not known was there. The neighbors who owned that part of the river had set up a fish cleaning table. This was a promising sign, so we made a note of the location.

We came to a stretch of river that looked the perfect spot for observation so we sat on a log for a while and discussed this new extension to our Secret Place. Since we had stopped hiking, it seemed a good idea to try our sandwiches. We did not intend to eat all our food, but it was quickly gone. We agreed there was nothing like a river hike to pep up the appetite, although breakfast was barely two hours past. I looked at my watch. It was ten forty five.

We resumed our trek into the new world with the enthusiasm of all pioneering folk. We explored a river bend and located some sand bars and found a log-free, swift flowing stretch of river just right for drum fishing.

At eleven fifteen, I was breaking tall weeds ahead of Steven; I stopped, turned to him and said, "Do you see what lies ahead of us?"

"Grandpa," he said, "I have been looking at it for a while, hoping it would go away."

It was the river bridge, a few hundred yards away. A car passed over it, going north, then an Amish horse and buggy. We could see the houses on the river bluffs that border the north edge of Cooks Mills.

We sat on a log at the edge of the Okaw and laughed. All our preparation, gear packing and planning for a trip that could have been covered in an hour! We don't know how we could have been in such great error on the timing and distance. Perhaps anticipation had been so great it overfed our imagination.

But we had a good laugh; we found a fishing hole and saw a new boat landing and unfamiliar river scenes. Most wonderful of all: we sighted what we believed to be a heron, one of those strange, long legged, fragile looking birds, seldom seen in our countryside.

Who cares whether an experience is lived in one hour or four hours, just so it is the stuff of which memories are built.

The Gathering of the Toads

AFTER EACH JOURNEY to the Secret Place, we discuss the happenings and decide which was the most exciting. One Friday afternoon we witnessed an event that headed our list for many days.

West of our house, half way between the lane's beginning and the old cemetery, there are two man-made ponds, dug to retain the liquid overflow from two nearby oil storage tanks. Each pond is approximately fifty feet square. The foul smelling liquid coming from the tanks flows through rusted iron pipes before emptying into the ponds and kills all vegetation for several feet around the banks, leaving a white deposit on the red clay as it evaporates.

The oil storage tanks are about fifteen feet high and their tops may be reached by climbing a sturdy metal ladder with hand rails. There is a wide metal platform running parallel to the tank tops and we can see the entire area of the Secret Place from this vantage point.

Looking west, we see the dark pines standing in the cemetery. To the east are the woods and the thicket where the quail hide out and, further east, the top of the cottonwood, showing over the crest of the hill.

South, the church roof is visible through the tall trees that hover around it and there is a glimpse of the roofs of Cooks Mills. A long line of dark trees marks the path of the river.

Turning north, we see the road that passes the haunted house and, on a clear day, the top of a grain elevator, eight miles away.

Our neighbor has erected a woven wire corn storage bin between the two oil tanks and the ponds. The corn bin stands even higher than the oil storage tanks. Ears of corn are conveyed into the top of the woven wire bin by a piece of equipment called a corn hiker. This has a belt that rolls the yellow ears to the top of the bin and drops them into storage. The hiker is left standing by the bin the year around and presents an obvious challenge to a pair of adventurers. Steven has seen the view from the top many times. I have always observed from the ground or the platform on the tank tops.

There is a woven metal, tunnel-shaped air duct running the diameter of the bin at the bottom. When the bin is bulging with the fall crop, we kneel at the entrance to the tunnel and watch rats run in the passage way. There are many of them and they are big and fat and unafraid. They glare back at us, from the dark of the tunnel, with little, red, evil eyes.

The ponds appeared void of any life form except for water bugs scooting across the surface. There were scores of these little black creatures and if we pitched a pebble near a swarm of them, they would scatter in a concentrated rush, then regroup and resume their aimless darting.

It seemed an unlikely spot for adventuring. However, we had the observation platform on the tanks and the corn hiker to climb on. The weeds sheltered birds and terrapins and snakes. More than once we saw the tall grasses ripple as some creature fled from our presence. There were many colonies of ants that could be observed on the banks and we held rock skipping contests across the water's surface. We spent many hours at those ponds.

One Friday afternoon we were watching the water bugs go about being water bugs and as we watched and idly skipped chunks of clay across the still surface, we were surprised to see a small pointed nose break through the water. A pair of eyes stared at us a moment, then the head sank from sight. It reappeared in a few seconds and, along side it, another head. Then we saw another, some distance away, then another. We realized those waters teemed with small turtles, each of which rose silently to the top, stared at us for a moment, then submerged. We thought this must be a hardy breed of turtles, especially the first one that took the plunge into those unlikely waters. Only a half mile from a river, and they begin life in those stagnant ponds surrounded by wasteland.

Darkness was closing in and we were without flashlights, so we returned home, talking of the new life we had encountered.

It was the following Friday before we could return to the pond and on that day we hurried to see if the turtles were still spending their days in that inhospitable environment.

As we climbed the low dyke that contains the west pond and walked to the water's edge, we saw a different form of life. Two small frogs were thrashing about in the shallows of the pond. One was astride the other's back. Then we saw another pair, then another. There were many pairs of frogs, coupled as in some bizarre mating ritual. We scooped a pair from the pond and discovered they were not frogs, they were toads, small, ugly toads. There were dozens of tiny toads meeting in the sluggish waters at this desolate place. We never concern ourselves with explanations of the happenings we see but we learned that toads do meet in shallow waters in mating time.

This was a gathering that had been prearranged in some natural, though mysterious, manner.

We remarked that had we been the toad in charge of arrangements we would have reserved some more romantic place of rendezvous.

It was at the ponds that we saw a poignant display of that strength for survival granted all wild things.

There are long lengths of metal pipe lying in the weeds and on the edges of the ponds. Each pipe is about five inches in diameter and twenty feet long. They were discarded years ago by some wasteful or careless construction crew.

Families of rats set up housekeeping in those pipes and it is great sport to tap the sides of the pipes with our staffs and watch the creatures spring from the pipe ends and scurry into the weeds. We talk of how their ears must ring as our staffs ping at the outside walls of their houses. We never tear out their nests and they are always back home when we return another day.

Once we tapped one of the pipes and a baby rat, no larger than my thumb, dropped from the opening and ran to the edge of the pond. We were close by and death must have seemed certain, so the little rat plunged without hesitation into the water and began swimming across the expanse that must have seemed to be endless.

Less than half way across the pond, instinct told the little thing that rats had not evolved for swimming great distances, so it changed course and paddled to the bank on its left.

It arrived at the water's edge and collapsed on the bank, exhausted. We picked it up; its sides heaved from the beating of its heart and its eyes were glazed with fear. When we gently set it in the weeds, it crawled into the undergrowth, its body leaving a trail of moisture.

We do not like rats of any size. They are unloved and unlovely. But this little creature made a gallant stand. It was a rat because it had been born a rat.

It had earned the right to survive.

The Case of the Silent Bull Frogs

MOST TOADS ARE not talkative. We have heard no songs or drumming from toads in our yard. But frogs are a different tribe altogether. Music is said to be merely organized sounds and if this is true, frogs are superb musicians. They demonstrate remarkable organization in their chatting and singing.

We have sat near the freshwater pond and listened as the frogs boomed at one another. Frogs are extremely polite in their conversation. One or two will sound off from a vantage point, then quickly quiet down so another frog in another place can contribute its remarks. If several speak simultaneously, there is a definite rhythm to the sounds. Each listening helps distinguish individual tones. We have often wondered how it was decided which frog was to speak first. Perhaps it is a matter of age, or size, or sex. As long as the frog knows, it should make little difference to the listener.

A family of bull frogs lived for several weeks across the road from our house. They had chosen a most unlikely spot in which to set up camp. They lived in a ditch in a little pool about the size of two bath tubs, half choked with cattails and small willow trees. A metal culvert had been crowded into the ditch and the frogs used this culvert as a hiding place.

Strangest fact of all, the pool was only thirty feet from the main travelled road, where cars and horses and buggies pass at all hours.

Most of the frog family was matured when we first noticed them. The weeds were so thick we would not have known of their presence if they had not made such awkward splashes as they retreated into the culvert.

It became a game to see how closely we could sneak up on them before they hid in the weeds or the culvert. Sometimes we could see just their heads and eyes as they patiently sat and waited for danger to pass.

We knew the little tribe had violated certain rules of frogdom. These rules were:

A. Live out your alloted days in a body of water large enough to allow escape.

B. That body of water should be as far removed from man as possible.

C. A frog should live in a place where it can sing and talk all it wishes.

Incredibly, in all the time those displaced frogs lived in the pool near our house, we never once heard a noise from the pool except the splashing. We sat on our patio at night and listened to the frog chorus echoing from the fresh water pond, but not once did we hear an answer from the little pond of water across the road.

Is it possible they knew a song in the night meant death for the singer? Frog legs are a delicacy here, as in other places.

We kept their secret. None but the frogs and we two ever knew the location of their home.

One day we crossed the road to visit the frogs and failed to hear the familiar, clumsy splashes. We clambered down the bank and looked into the long muddy culvert. We probed the weeds and cattails with our staffs and searched the ditch but they were gone, and we were glad.

We wondered if they had realized how ridiculously vulnerable they were, so near the road. Perhaps they sat in their shallow pond at night and listened to the deep bass calls of their friends down by the river and had decided that life without song is not life at all for a frog.

Who knows why they left? As long as the frog knows, it will survive.

Like man, domesticated animals worry a lot. Perhaps they worry because of man. Pigs are said to develop ulcers. Horses nervously chew at wooden stalls and feeding troughs; and any chicken farmer can tell of the mass hysteria that occasionally sweeps through a flock.

We believe that wild things do not worry, they fear. However, they possess the enviable facility of fearing only when there is something to fear. Man has never been capable of separating his real fears from his imagined ones, but wild things can. A rabbit will flee in panic from a hunter and his dog but seconds after danger has passed will hop around, contentedly chewing clover stems. A fox plays a deadly game of tag with the dog pack but after the pack has gone its way, the fox goes calmly about its business without an apparent thought of the next pack.

Nothing seems to worry a frog a great deal although it faces death in two worlds. A frog has hungry enemies on land and in the water.

A frog's every move, even the fearful ones, seem calculated. It will wait until we are almost upon it before it squeals and plunges into the safety of the water. The leap may be timed so we are far enough from the frog to make grabbing it impossible, yet close enough that we are startled by the sudden movement.

Faced with something it doesn't understand, the frog will wait long moments, unblinking and motionless, before it makes its move. It will outwait any living thing until the right pyschological moment.

One afternoon Steven and I saw a huge specimen squatting at the edge of a little stream that wanders through several meadows before feeding the river. We were staring down at the frog from a wooden plank bridge. It knew we were there and it also knew we could not reach it as long as we stayed on the bridge. Its decision was to wait us out.

We found a length of discarded fishing line and Steven caught a big brown grasshopper. We tied the grasshopper to the fishing line and dangled the wildly kicking creature inches from the big bull's nose. It sat as unmoving and unblinking as a carved frog. We pulled the grasshopper up and set it free and it hopped off to live another day. We don't know if frogs find grasshoppers unappetizing or if instinct told the frog that sudden movement meant disaster.

We began dropping pebbles and chunks of dirt close to where the big frog sat staring across the little stream. None struck its body though some came very close. Yet the bull sat as unflinching as though being pelted with pebbles were a part of its normal routine.

We were struck with the ridiculous thought that perhaps it was not that the frog wouldn't move, maybe it couldn't move. Wild creatures are probably as susceptible to as many aches and pains and crippling diseases as man. Colds, toothaches and sore feet may be a part of their lives, even as ours.

We decided to climb down the weed-covered bank and investigate, but the instant we began our descent toward the frog it leaped far out into the water and disappeared. The frog knew its business well. It had ignored the indignities we had heaped on it but when real danger threatened, it knew to act. It was in control of the situation.

A small frog gave us a rare glimpse of death from natural causes in the Secret Place.

We marvel at the neatness with which mother nature keeps house. We seldom see the remains of any wild creature that has perished from what is called a "natural death." Surely, not all animals meet violent, untimely ends, but it seems so. It would stretch even our imaginations to think of the wild things that we observe as passing away of old age. Death was causd by violence in most of the bodies we have found, and death is normally caused by that great motivator, hunger. In the Secret Place the pattern is hunger, search, stalk, kill, eat. Nothing must be left on the plate and if a few bits remain the scavengers move in and clean up.

So it is that we happen across few signs of death on our walks. Death and violence travel together but they leave little evidence of their passing. A few drops of blood, a lone feather or a swatch of rabbit fur and we know there has been a vicious rush, a moment of terror and a cry of despair. One lives, the other dies and the pattern has been followed.

It was unusual we should discover Caruso, our frog, in such well preserved condition.

It was a late afternoon and we had begun a hike through the woods to the pond. We climbed a barbed wire fence and stopped awhile to observe a pool of water in a shallow depression just beyond the fence. Dozens of tadpoles had buried themselves in the silt on the bottom of the miniature pond. We discovered that if we wiggled our staffs into the mud and stirred it around, the little creatures zig-zagged across the surface in desperate flight, although there was really no hiding place. After scattering through the water in all directions, the wrigglers would settle back down into the muck and resume doing whatever a tadpole does until we stirred the mud again.

Steven saw Caruso first, a flash of white in the murky waters of the little pool. He reached in and pulled out a very small and a very dead frog. It had been lying on the bottom on its back with its legs outstretched, its head thrown back and its mouth opened wide. It was the white underside of its belly that had shown through the water. There were no marks of violence and we wondered what frogs die of, if not from old age or predators. Its strained posture and wide opened mouth reminded us of a singer in a tense moment of attempting a difficult note.

"We will call it Caruso," I said.

"Who is Caruso, Grandpa?"

I told the boy as much as I knew of the golden voiced singer. Many years ago I had visited with a friend whose father owned a collection of Caruso records. The records were scratchy and imperfect but through the imperfections one could still appreciate that magnificent voice.

We propped little Caruso against a piece of bark we found lying nearby and left him sitting there with his legs outstretched and his mouth still opened wide. His songs would remain forever unsung.

The next morning Caruso was gone. We searched around the pool but there was no trace of our frog and we knew the cleanup squad had been at work. The plan had been carried out and the law of cleanliness obeyed.

Creative Watching

EACH MOVEMENT, EACH object may pose a threat to survival for the wild things. We know each creature in the Secret Place is well aware of our presence long before we reach its territory. This is the reason we need to be silent and still while we are observing in the woods. We are watched by many more wild things than we are privileged to see.

A bough may sway with the wind without disturbing the routine of a busy squirrel, but movement from one of us can send the same squirrel scampering to the other side of its tree. If we sit a little longer in the same place, the squirrel will peek its head around the tree trunk to see if the alien presence is still there. Animals are fearful and mistrustful of out-of-place objects, but they are also inquisitive.

We will sit on a log and as the long moments pass without a movement or sound from either of us, we begin to be accepted as a new but harmless part of the world. Life begins.

As the routines and happenings start afresh, a little imagination helps create a new perspective to an old world. It becomes a fascinating game to fit words and thoughts to the actions of the wild things.

One Thursday afternoon I was picking up walnuts under the tall old trees that shade the cabin atop the river bluffs.

As I bent to my task, I heard the hoarse squawk of a male pheasant. The cock pheasant sounds a harsh, off-key call, contrasting oddly with its brilliant plumage. I assumed some careless pheasant had made its last move a fraction late and, even now, a fox was taking home its dinner.

I straightened from the pile of walnuts I was sacking and, standing motionless, looked in the direction from which the sound came.

As I watched, a handsome red fox crossed the brow of a grassy knoll, stopped suddenly, and stared back at me. It was not carrying a pheasant, so perhaps the fox was the one whose move had been a fraction late. I was too far away for it to catch my scent or even to see me clearly, but it knew something was where it should not have been and it was concerned.

We think it possible the wild things know the location of each object in their territory as we know the furnniture in our houses.

We stood staring, neither of us moving. The fox cocked its head to one side in the manner of a puppy or kitten and studied me intently.

Presently there was a movement to the right of the puzzled animal and another fox slowly walked across the same rise in the meadow. It stood at the shoulder of the first fox and stared at me just as intently. It could have been a ridiculous scene, two foxes and a human staring at each other with intensity.

It was easy to create the imagined conversation.

"Do you see it?"

"Yes, but what is it? There was nothing beside that walnut tree this morning."

"Maybe that is what scared my pheasant."

"You lost the pheasant because of your clumsy stalking. If I could hear you thrashing through the weeds, how could you expect to surprise a pheasant? Do I need to remind you we haven't eaten anything today?"

The pair of foxes turned and slowly walked away, looking back over their shoulder occasionally.

This may sound ridiculous but, remember, the Secret Place is only half real and those who think animals are unable to communicate have never shared a Secret Place.

The lone crow sitting on a fence post and cawing sporadically is on the post for a reason. Move a little closer to its perch and listen to the changed tone of its calls and see the rest of its tribe flap to safety. The sentinel has sounded the alarm.

Walk among the trees at the river's edge and note how quickly the birds' conversations cease after a warning whistle has sounded.

A bee keeper told us that scout bees locate the field where the work will be done that day, then return and employ a set dancing pattern to tell the workers of the location.

We are frequently accompanied to the river by a small bird that fancies itself a comic. As we plod, earth bound, down the slope of the hill, this fellow flies a few feet above our heads. As it flies it sounds what can best be described as an inane giggle.

"Tee Hee...Tee Hee...Tee Hee..." it goes as it darts back and forth.

We pretend it follows us to make light of our slow walk as it wheels above us, seeing sights we can only imagine.

One afternoon we paused by the old tractor to rest and to observe awhile.

My hair has been white for some years now and I rarely wear a hat as we hike.

As we sat and talked of many things, a little bird fluttered to a tree branch, inches above our heads. It bent its head slightly forward and its sharp little eyes studied us carefully.

Suddenly, it screeched a word and fled toward the tall trees in the woods.

Steven turned to me and I could see he was laughing.

"Grandpa, did you hear what that bird said?"

"Tell me, Steven, and let's see if we heard the same word."

"Just as plain as anything, it yelled 'Snow' before it flew."

"That's exactly what I thought it said."

We wondered if the bird went to its friends and told them of the patch of snow it had seen in August. Did its tale cause excitement and concern or did it get hooted out of the flock for its absurd story? None of the bird's tribe came to take a look so we imagined its message was considered just another tall tale.

An animal occasionally suffers a lapse of instinct, even in the presence of man.

We wondered if the bird went to its friends and told them of the patch of snow it had seen in August. Did its tale cause excitement and concern or did it get hooted out of the flock for its absurd story? None of the bird's tribe came to take a look so we imagined its messge was considered just another tall tale.

An animal occasionally suffers a lapse of instinct, even in the presence of man.

One day Steven was standing on the river bank a short distance from where I was fishing. As he stood and watched the flow of the river, he heard a rhythmic thumping sound, like something running.

A plump groundhog scurried past Steven. The hog's nose was close to the ground and its legs worked frantically in its haste. It vanished into a clump of weeds; it was obvious it had not noticed the boy's presence, although it had passed within six feet of him.

In a matter of seconds, there was a second running sound and another groundhog hurried along the same path as the first and vanished into the same clump of weeds. It, too, had completely overlooked the presence of man.

It must have been a matter of great importance to have caused both groundhogs to forget the unforgettable.

But, then, why should there not be absent-minded groundhogs? If man, with his highly developed brain, strays from routine thinking, it is probable that animals do the same. Forgetfulness is surely not confined to one tribe in the plan of things.

One would think the snake family would be the most alert of all wild things. Their enemies are legion and they live most of their days in hiding. They are said to be sensitive to ground vibrations and weed movement and they count no object as a friendly one. However, not even snakes are as cautious as they need to be.

Steven and I were sitting on the cabin porch one early afternoon. The cabin sits on a high bluff above the river and from our vantage point we could see far upstream. The sun warmed our faces and a breeze fluttered the leaves. Thor, the hawk, circled above the meadow to our west in his constant, floating search. A spider waited for its meal in a web close to our feet. It had tied one end of its trap close to the big metal plate that lies in front of the cabin porch, and we sat watching to see what prey would find its way into the thin threads of the web.

Suddenly, a garden snake poked its head through a

hole in the metal plate and stiffened a part of its body a good four inches straight up in the air. It looked like a stick with a pointed end and it made no more movement than a stick. Then, very, very slowly it moved its head from side to side and its little eyes studied the ground and the bushes ahead of it as its tongue nervously licked and thrust. When its head had turned one hundred eighty degrees to the left, it would remain in that position for long moments, then slowly, slowly turn its head until had completed a half circle to the right.

We don't know how great a distance a snake can see nor its capability for recognizing objects but this one did not move for at least five minutes. Was it memorizing its surroundings? Was it planning an avenue of escape? Was it hunting?

The only flaw in its cautious behavior was that not once did it look where we sat, barely two feet away. It didn't look behind it! We could have crushed its head with our staffs at any time.

A leaf fell, the spider ran the length of its web and back again to its waiting place, a bush rustled with a passing breeze. The snake remained motionless through all the happenings, although it could see them as well as we.

At long last, satisfied there was no danger nearby, it slithered the rest of its eighteen inch body through the hole in the metal plate and moved into the ravine, quickly disappearing into the leaf blanket covering the slope.

Foolish, careless snake. It had never seen us. Is this how and why most wild things die?

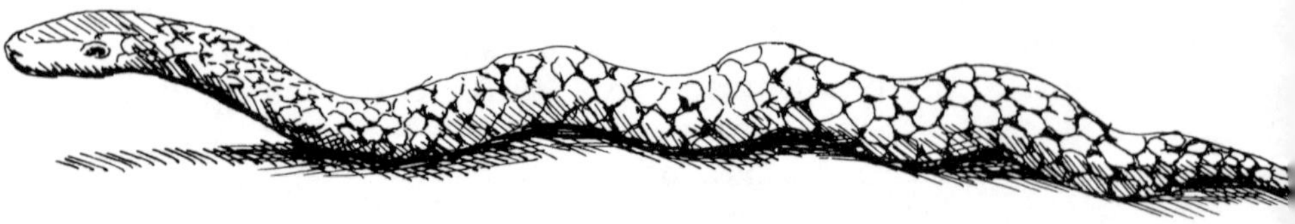

We Make a Friend

WE PAY LITTLE attention to domesticated animals on our hikes. Sometimes we poke fresh green grass through the woven wire fence to feed the Amish Dutchman's horses. Although the green grass is identical on their side of the fence, the big animals come to us eagerly, as though we are offering a rare dessert. We watch the white faced bull that lives with his harem in the pasture near the old cemetery. We watch him from a respectful distance. Once, he became interested in our activities and we retreated across the fence and through a briar patch. It was an ignoble retreat, but a common sense one.

We are interested in those creatures that feel no kinship with man, rather than those who spend their days serving him.

However, we formed a special friendship with a dog and that friendship has lasted to this day.

We first met him on a late afternoon. We were walking north along the river path, going to the campsite. The daylight loses its battle with darkness quickly under the trees along the bank of a river and the shadows were beginning to form on the path behind us.

Suddenly we heard the sounds of running coming from the darkest of those shadows. It was obviously a large animal creating the sounds and, whatever it was, it was coming directly toward us. Each of us later confessed we had felt some concern, for we had heard talk of dog packs and sheep killing.

In a few seconds, the animal itself emerged from the dark beneath the trees and hurtled across a clearing toward us. It was one of the largest dogs we had ever seen. Its mouth was spread wide and its teeth shone in the half light. It was black except for a white patch on its breast and white spots on its legs.

Its thick tail was furiously circling. It was glad to see us.

Throughout the years the big black dog has always been glad to see us. We do not deceive ourselves that we are the only humans he is glad to see. He is glad to see anybody, any time, anywhere. He is a dog that enjoys, just enjoys.

We never know how he senses we are there, but he meets us at the river bend where the willows touch the water. He is eager for new adventures and walks home with us at the end of the day.

He is enthusiastic about anything that happens and if nothing is happening, he remains enthusiastic. He likes swimming, running and walking and anything that takes place in between. From the looks of his tattered ears and scarred head, he even enjoys fighting.

Our friend is a heavy breather. He huffs and puffs with the least exertion, and his panting can be heard a great distance.

The big, black dog is a clumsy animal. Instead of running through the weeds and underbrush, he crashes through. We have seen him sit for awhile on the river bank, admiring his kingdom, and then turn and trip over a tree root. He spends a great deal of time paddling around in the river and we are never certain whether it is by choice or if he has fallen in.

What he likes most of all is to get close. He presses as closely as possible to us as we stand by the bank or sit by our campfire. After he has swum awhile or rolled in the mud, he will come and rub against us and whine as though he were frightened of things we cannot see. This is nothing but an act for that dog has never been frightened of anything in its entire life.

In the manner of all dogs, the big, black one likes to "look noble." Dogs assume this expression when they are with people whom they love. They will hunch down at the feet of the human they are with and stare off into the distance with lifted head and brooding eyes. They pretend they are thinking grand thoughts and recalling heroic dog deeds.

Our friend is not always a clumsy clown. He is a hunter and a killer.

We have a deep respect for the wild things that live in the Secret Place. However, we know those lives are not always pleasant for there is hunger and there is hunting and there is death.

Once, after we had known him awhile, the dog met us at the top of the hill by the gatepost and the three of us started down the slope toward the bend in the river. The dog ranged ahead, investigating and marking his territory.

He suddenly stiffened and froze into a magnificent black and white statue. His nose was pointed toward a clump of reddish brown weeds that huddled at the base of a crabapple tree and he began to tremble with excitement.

"Steven," I whispered, "he has spotted a rabbit. Now, watch, when the rabbit makes its move, it will run directly under that barbed and woven wire fence, and through the middle of that blackberry patch."

Fences and briar patches are a rabbit's best friends. They may offer a second or two delay that could mean survival, for while a dog is struggling through or over a fence, the rabbit has escaped into the meadow or woods.

The statue burst into action and hurled itself at the clump of weeds. A rabbit bounded from the base of the crabapple tree, barely a foot ahead of the big black dog, streaked through the fence and its white tail disappeared into the briar patch. The dog crashed through the briars in pursuit, making enough noise for many dogs, with a great deal of barking and howling.

The rabbit eluded the dog somewhere in that tangle of weeds and briars and Steven breathed a sigh of relief.

However, we knew we should not be overly optimistic. Rabbits follow an often fatal habit of running in circles and returning to their starting place. Rabbits, like humans, like to be home in times of danger. Hunters know this and dogs know this.

The dog was close behind. The dog was not barking, it was running in silent fury.

We never knew if the unfortunate rabbit miscalculated the size of the fence opening or if it was tired from the chase, for rabbits are very short winded; but it never made it through the woven wire. It made its leap for the life-giving fence but was momentarily slowed by one of the strands.

The dog caught up and that last precious second of timing was lost. The big jaws closed around the struggling body, there was a choked-off scream, the dog flipped its head, and the rabbit dangled lifeless, its neck broken.

We didn't stay to see the finish. The dog joined us later.

Rabbits sometimes win.

Once we stood on the hill by the cabin where I had stared down the two foxes. We were watching the black dog hunt in the meadow to the west of us.

He seemed to know what he was doing. He zig-zagged in a constant run across the short meadow grass, with his nose close to the ground. He stopped frequently, standing motionless, head held high, eyes searching the weeds and bushes ahead of him. He would slowly approach a growth of shrubs, stand for a moment, then resume his criss-crossing trot. Our friend was not the buffoon we knew, tripping over tree roots and falling into the river. He never glanced in our direction, but kept at his relentless search.

A row of wind-break—oak and maple and hickory—trees stands north of the sassafrass and west of the field where the dog was hunting. The ground beneath the trees grows thick with tickle grass, spanish needles and briars. A tumble-down fence dissects the copse, north and south. Birds and wild things shelter in that row of trees, for possible escape is offered by the cornfield to the west, or the meadow to the east or the deep ravine to the north. We think the creatures choose their resting places carefully, selecting those that offer more than one avenue of escape.

We saw a rabbit move cautiously on the crest of the hill near the sassafrass, hop ever so slowly along the line of trees and go directly into one of the briar patches. It was going north, just out of the dog's line of vision. If the rabbit had moved swiftly, the motion would have attracted the dog's attention.

We saw the rabbit emerge from the south end of the trees a few moments later and crouch behind a bush at the north end of the sassafrass. It had travelled north among the oaks and maples and doubled back south. This is an age-old trick employed by all rabbits.

In a few moments the dog arrived at the clump of weeds that had first sheltered the rabbit and, nose still to the ground, broke into a swift pace. Then he plunged, with full cry, into the weeds and trees.

The instant the dog ran north, sounding the chase, the rabbit moved further south, and crossed a small ravine. It was still unhurried and we smiled at each other as we saw it cross the fence into the horse pasture, many yards to the south.

The dog came running to us later, breathing heavily and begging for attention, as though he were to be congratulated for an heroic deed. Dogs are never embarrassed by their failures.

We discovered the big dog could also be gentle.

At certain times of the year, the river bank is home for a multitude of small frogs. They hop through the weeds and across the mud banks and splash into the river ahead of us as we hike. None is longer than two inches and we don't know if they are baby bull frogs or of some other species. We reason this is a hatching time, if there is such a time, and we wonder what becomes of them when they mature. Such large numbers of adult frogs would be noticeable, indeed. They are there a few days, leaping and splashing and then they are gone. We don't know if they meet death from predators in the Secret Place or if there is a mass migration to another place.

As we neared the river on this particular day, the dog was so intent on a game he was playing he didn't rush to meet us as usual. At times he would slap at the ground as a kitten plays with a ball. At other times, he would cant his head, study something with intensity, then leap at that something and snap at it with his huge mouth. Sometimes, his leaps would carry him off the bank and into the river, where he would continue his pouncing and snapping in the water.

We realized the dog was catching the tiny frogs. It was a little saddening to see our mighty hunter reduced to stalking and dining on small frogs.

Then we saw the wonderful thing that was happening. As quickly as he snapped one of the little things, the big dog would set the terrified creature back on the ground and leap for another. The released frog would hop away unhurt, but in an understandable hurry.

The big dog wasn't hungry. He was playing games.

In spite of his muscled bulk and his superb fighting equipment, we have never seen the big dog in an irritable mood. One day a guest was with us on a hike. A guest that must have sorely tried a friend's patience.

A small white dog lives near our house and its dearest wish is to walk to the river with us. Many times it has asked to go with us by running down the lane behind us or walking alongside us as though that was what we expected of it. We discourage it by throwing rocks near it or scolding and pointing towards its home. Our threatening gestures are taken as friendly overtures and, even while we are scolding most furiously, it will stand in the center of the lane, with its tongue hanging out and its tail wagging wildly, as though it were enjoying a game with us.

We sneak off down the lane a few times when the dog isn't looking, although we feel like children avoiding the unpopular kid on the block. It is not that we dislike the little fellow but the truth is, he is very noisy and we also wonder what the big, black dog would think of him.

The fuzzy dog's principal weapons are sound and fury. When Amish wagons, pulled by huge, well-fed work horses, rattle down the road, the little animal attacks the wheels and the horses' hooves. Its teeth are bared to the gums and its barks border on hysteria. Although neither the Amishman nor the horses show much concern over the attacks, the dog returns to its favorite resting place by the smokehouse after the wagon has rumbled on down the road. It flops down and assumes a look of pride. Once again, courage in a small package has triumphed.

Even wind-blown leaves and pieces of paper are

subject to the little dog's wrath, and it will pursue these with the same bravery it shows in attacking horses.

On this day the little dog was so persistent that we were losing valuable hiking time trying to send it home; we allowed him to walk with us to the Place.

It soon became apparent that we were not to see much wild life on this trip. Each stray leaf must be pursued and barked at, each sound in the woods must be loudly investigated. The big dog's clumsiness was more subtle than the little one's noisy curiosity. It listened to our scolding with friendly enthusiasm and we failed to make clear how one behaves in the Secret Place.

While we were discussing ways to protect the little dog without hurting the big one's feelings, we heard the unmistakable sounds of our friend's approach. He was running toward us with his usual enthusiasm.

The little white pup exploded into a frenzy of activity. Its offense consisted of a series of rushes, each of which stopped just short of body contact. After each rush it would retreat and stand beside us and fill the air with threats and insults.

Not once did it retreat to a position behind us and we realized the little creature thought it was protecting us from the big black enemy. We felt a touch of shame at the memory of how we had treated the little dog on other days. An act of imagined heroism requires as much courage as the real thing.

We were proud of the big, black dog that day. He endured the pup's loud activity for a while, then came over to us and asked for a pat on the head. After accepting our greetings, he slowly walked over to the ashes of a previous campfire, seated himself with great dignity and opened his mouth in an enormous yawn.

We managed to soothe the smaller dog and after a few awkward moments, the big black one stood up, trotted to the river's edge, plunged in, swam to the opposite shore, and went home.

Perhaps our neighbor's dog thinks of this adventure as it lies by the smoke house waiting for horses to intimidate. It may proudly recall that heroic moment when it stood between its two friends and danger.

The big, black dog is not a perfect pet dog. He wheezes a great deal. At times he has an odor and he is host for ticks and fleas and millions of gnats. He is clumsy and he is overly friendly. However, he loves us and approves of all we do. We could not ask for more.

Beauty Blind

IT TAKES MORE than sight, sound and silence to experience a world like the Secret Place. Fantasy must be mixed well with reality.

We were under the trees at the river's edge late on a summer afternoon. We had agreed it was time to return home to popcorn and cold drinks.

The shadows of the outside row of trees, next to the meadow, had already joined those of the trees nearest the river to cast dark shapes on the water's surface. The song birds had quieted and the cattle in the pasture across the Okaw had begun walking their well-worn paths toward the feeding bunks. In the distance, two mourning doves were calling each other softly and sadly; they, too, would soon settle in for the night.

We rose from the log on which we had been sitting and walked through the trees to the edge of the meadow. It was a magic moment there and we were reluctant to leave.

We heard the sounds of a squirrel, hurtling itself from branch to branch, coming toward us. In a few moments, we saw it; we had never seen a squirrel in such a hurry. It raced so intently through the trees it forgot the basic law of survival, ignoring the two of us who stood in the midst of a little clearing.

It made a long, spectacular leap to a shaggy barked hickory tree directly to our right, scampered up the trunk and popped into a nest on the topmost branches.

Perhaps this was a squirrel frightened of the approaching darkness since it is reasonable to assume that animals, like people, feel safest at home on a dark night.

Or it could be a squirrel with a wife waiting in that nest; a wife who had issued an ultimatum about any more late dinners.

Maybe this was a squirrel that had stopped off for a chat with the boys at his favorite hickory nut tree and we all know how time flies when one is enjoying pleasant company.

We feel a touch of compassion for those who would have seen only a squirrel leaping from tree to tree.

Other people seldom accompany us on our hikes, for the Secret Place is to be shared only with those who can see and believe the unbelievable. When Steven was small and the fantasies more real than now, he was always worried about eavesdroppers and intruders.

Once, years ago, we were near our campsite and the Amishman who lives north of the sassafras grove chanced into our territory. Since he is a friend and a good neighbor, I chatted with him awhile and enjoyed our visit. However, Steven left his vine-swinging and sat on a log near us and spoke only when spoken to. I knew what was on the boy's mind and after my Amish friend had left, I reminded Steven there are those who do not see or hear, whatever the happening. Just because a thing happens doesn't mean it is understood.

One of Steven's friends hiked to the Place with us one Saturday afternoon. He was a pleasant companion and we enjoyed his company.

Both afternoons were full for observing, and there was much going on but our friends missed almost everything.

They never noticed the weeds ripple nor heard them rustle as Mrs. Green or one of her tribe fled from us. They never once focused binoculars on Thor, the hawk, wheeling overhead. Our friends were too concerned about tripping over tree roots or running into Spanish needle bushes to watch the effortless and incredibly beautiful flight. When we sat on the logs the talk was constant; the animals listened in silence and none ventured out to be observed.

They did not notice the strident warning whistle of the birds as we approached their grove of trees, nor the silence of the song birds as we passed nor that they began their calling and singing after we had left their territory.

Steven and I discussed this experience at a campfire and we came to the conclusion that we were the ones at fault. We had become snobs with our observing and our Place and we should not have expected our friends to know our rules for observation.

However, we continued to take our trips alone.

The Sounds of Death

ONE WHO LOVES the outdoor life understands the exhilaration of hunting. The nip in the air on a fine autumn day. The camaraderie of sportsmen. The quickening of the pulse as a pheasant explodes skyward. The performance of a finely balanced gun in the hands of a sportsman. Each of these contribute to a special sensation that has thrilled man since the days he stalked and killed from necessity.

There are arguments that selective hunting controls game overpopulation problems. This may be true, but we have seen the ugly side of hunting on our hikes.

We have seen wild things slaughtered and left lying in our meadow by hunters more interested in the skills of dealing death than in salvaging what they have killed. A downed, half-dead quail or pheasant is not easy to find in tall weeds, and it is easier to move to the next kill than to spend time looking for the present victim.

We have seen rabbits with half their bodies shot away by some inept sportsman who has blasted at close range or shot the animal head on. We have seen the bodies of song birds mangled by buckshot.

We hear the thunder of guns around the Secret Place in hunting season and we wonder if the squirrel we saw in the trees yesterday is playing there today.

Steven and I started a hike to the river on a beautiful fall day. There was a crispness in the air that caused us to walk a little faster than usual; and a light snow the previous night had dusted the bushes and grass. The sky was the pale blue of a pool of deep water. It was a good day to be alive.

It was to be a day of death for many of the wild things in the Secret Place for we had heard the sound of the guns all morning.

We thought we might sight a covey of quail in the blackberry patch at the side of the lane. I had seen them there the day before and perhaps they would sleep late on this chilly morning before venturing into the field to scavenge kernels of corn left by the picker. Wild things sleep in late some mornings, just like humans.

We reached the thicket with its tangle of briars and weeks and stood staring silently into the thick underbrush. Neither of us moved. Presently, we heard them moving nervously about and making tiny peeping noises. They didn't take flight and, as the long moments passed, we could see them quite clearly although they were camouflaged in the browned leaves.

We walked on, our breath fogging the cold air ahead of us.

We met a party of hunters at the top of our hill. Each sportsman was well armed and each carried a bulging game bag.

One asked if we had located any quail and I replied that we had. I could feel Steven stiffen as he stood beside me, looking at me in disbelief.

"Why don't you look over there?" I said, pointing directly away from the covey.

As soon as the hunters were out of hearing, Steven whispered, "Thanks, Grandpa."

It is certain that the gods of chase and of hunters will never forgive my deception, but perhaps the patron saint of all wild things heard and understood and smiled.

We have placed the thought in our minds that the animals we observe know us and count us as friends although reality tells us this thinking is impossible thinking. But it is very pleasant thinking.

As we sit on our big log by the fire, watching the happenings, we tell ourselves that there are many pairs of eyes watching us. also. They watch us from their hiding places in the weeds and bushes and up in the trees, and they wonder and they fear. In truth, a wild thing knows that to trust anything is to die.

Gunshots are not the only sounds of death in the Secret Place. We have heard the high pitched squeal of a frog and a rabbit's scream. Each met death at a woven wire fence or by the water's edge.

Once we heard a sound of dying few humans will ever hear.

We watched the big hawk on many of our trips to the river. We named it Thor and we consider it an old friend. It circles above us as we descend the hill to the meadow then glides, scarcely moving its wings, to another part of the sky. We have stood under the trees at the meadow's edge and watched Thor soar and wheel and dive, then glide upward again.

One cool day in early spring, we observed our friend in flight for awhile, then turned back to the campsite to stir up our fire and warm our feet.

As we sat and talked, we were startled by a sound from the meadow. It was a cry of terror or of pain. It was a cry of despair. It was a penetrating sound and even in the daylight by the warmth of our fire and in familiar surroundings, there was a ring to the sound that caused us to sit in shocked silence for a fraction of a second.

Turning quickly, we looked through the lower branches of the trees and could see Thor rising from the meadow with a struggling body in its talons. We could see the victim's death-thrashings until the big hawk soard out of sight.

We have heard that a hunting bird, such as the hawk, will screech loudly a second or so before impact in order to paralyze its victim with fear.

We think what we heard was not the sound of the hunter. It was the sound of death.

A Beast Called Man
By Steven at age 13

As I stand in silence, watching river life among the trees, I wonder what the young squirrel sees...when man comes and destroys its home, to make paper and homes for some.

And the fish as he banquets in the brook and is suddenly jagged by the fisherman's hook ...and cannot, for the life of him understand this cruel and unusual beast called man.

And the deer, while running through the wood, is shot down painfully and in cold bood and wonders why...on his own land, he is killed by such as this beast called man.

And the quail, while in flight from field to field...is shot down because man would not yield. . . and falls needlessly to the land, at the will of the superior beast called man.

And when the symbol of peace and love. . . is shot for sport, as is the dove. . . then the situation is out of hand and there is ho hope for the beast called man.

Games

MOST PEOPLE ASSUME that the lives and actions of wild things are governed only by instinct. This is to say that hunger, sleep, propagation and survival occupy each moment of the animal's life. There would be no remaining moments for such emotions as love, loyalty and humor. However, we have seen creatures in the Secret Place do things that could never be explained by that cold word, instinct.

We have noticed that the weather has a great deal to do with the numbers of wild life we are privileged to observe. In dry times, when the leaves are brittle underfoot and the weeds are brown and thirsty, we know most of the action will cease long before we can watch any happenings. We have announced our presence by the noise we make. We practice walking silently, heel down first, then toes placed gently and slowly, but there is the inevitable snapping of twigs and rustling of dry leaves. Even the rabbit can be heard on those days, for long after its little white cottontail has bobbed from sight, we track its run by the sounds it makes in such underbrush. How does the hunter stalk the hunted on such days? A full stomach depends on the element of surprise.

Animals and birds alike are slow starters on cold days, delaying flight until the last possible moment. We are often startled by the leap of a rabbit almost from underfoot.

One day, we circled the maple grove and struck out across the meadow toward the campsite. Although this particular spot of ground is thick with spanish needles and tickle grass, we take this route to avoid the poison ivy growing along the outer row of river trees.

We were a scant dozen steps from the shade of the maple grove when a frantic fluttering rustled the weeds ahead of us.

We stopped and waited.

It was a bird about the size of a robin and it was in obvious distress. Its left wing dangled helplessly and its stiffened right leg appeared altogether useless. It could neither run nor fly but dragged itself along in a pitiable crawl. As we advanced toward the crippled creature, it managed to keep a distance of ten to twelve feet between us and itself, at all times. When we paused, it stopped its dragging but continued to flutter, and when we resumed our advance, it managed to gather enough strength to remain ahead of us.

Steven smiled at me and said, "Quite an act, Grandpa." We knew that as soon as the mother bird had lured us away from her nest, hidden somewhere in that tangle of grasses, she would rise in perfect flight. She was wagering her life that we would follow her instead of looking for her nest.

We decided to wait her out so we stood as motionless as one of the maples. She stopped as we stopped, pivoted helplessly in the grass and watched us intently. When she saw we were not chasing her, the little actress limped and fluttered for a few more feet, then soared easily into the air and to the cottonwood, where she perched on the lowest limb and began loudly scolding us.

We left her and walked back through the meadow, taking care we did not step on the nest and the little ones.

We hid beneath the leafy branches and watched. She did not return to her nest until she could no longer see us.

We like to think that mother love and not unthinking instinct or evolution provided the inspiration for that beautiful, unselfish act.

Wild animals play games. They play deadly games, with survival as the prize. A fox plays games with the hounds, leading them on an exhausting chase, back-tracking, water-wading and log-leaping. Those who believe animals cannot gloat should watch a fox trot home as the dogs circle a cold trail and yell and curse at each other.

We saw the big, black dog lose a game of tag.

We had walked the river bank past the willows and around the bend. We had not stopped at the campsite but had hiked almost to the cabin. We sat for a while on a log that had been washed ashore many years ago.

There were few happenings and we were ready to call it a day. Thor was hunting in another part of his territory. The fish lay at the bottom of the river; none had leaped since we had been observing. Even the squirrels were in hiding.

The big dog joined us and crowded close awhile, concerned that we were not moving about. Once, he ran off into the woods in pursuit of something only he could see, but gave up the chase and came to sit beside us and wheeze, as was his custom. We left our observation log and walked toward the cabin. It was a lazy day.

Suddenly, a muskrat plunged into the river from the bank ahead of us. Instead of seeking refuge in the roots of the over-hanging trees, this big fellow swam out to the river channel and slowly paddled back and forth, in plain sight. Rats are strong, swift swimmers and will normally disappear under the surface when frightened, to reappear far down stream. They are diligent workers and we have watched through binoculars many times as they patrolled the banks and water's edge. We have never understood just what they are doing to stay so busy, but they keep fast pace.

The big dog is normally an observant animal and few movements escape his notice but, although we pointed and shouted and encouraged him, it was some time before he realized what we were trying to tell him.

Eventually he saw the rat swimming back and forth and he leaped into the water with an heroic shout. Unbelievably, the rat maintained its swimming pattern and in a matter of seconds, the dog was within fighting distance.

But the rat had set the rules for this game and knew those rules well; when the dog came within three feet of it, it disappeared beneath the surface and the dog was swimming alone. Almost immediately, the rat reappeared ten feet behind the big dog and began swimming back and forth again. The dog switched directions and, again, as soon as the rat had allowed a distance of three feet, it dived, to reappear in another area, ten feet away.

This mismatched game was played for several

moments, but at last the dog realized it was outclassed. It swam to shore, shook itself vigorously, allowed itself a defiant bark, then came to us to be complimented on its fine performance. The big dog lives a life of positive attitudes and always considers itself the hero of any situation.

We thought the rat looked pleased with itself as it paddled off downstream.

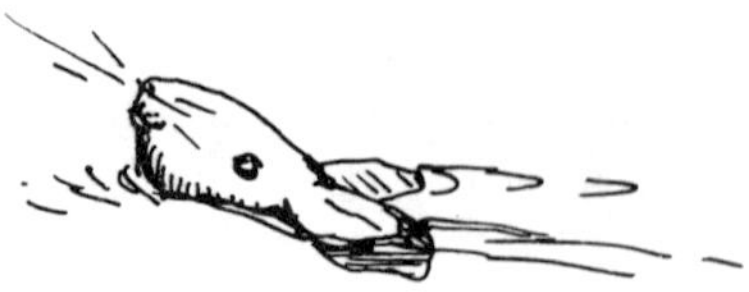

The Old House

THERE ARE FEW times when our adventures take us any great distance from the Secret Place. The mile-square area we explore holds enough wonders to occupy all the hours we can spare.

There are a rich variety of happenings on the acre on which our house sits. The comings and goings in the ant cities may be studied. We use a magnifying glass to watch the activity in the hills and tunnels. After observing close up the fighting equipment carried as part of an ant's body, we feel grateful the little creatures have not evolved into a larger size. We try to imagine the peril of poking our staffs into a hole filled with cat-sized ants. If the cousins of the ants, the termites, had evolved into a larger size they would be fearsome enemies, indeed.

We sit on the patio and listen to the domestic squabbles of the families of robins.

There is a continuing battle between the sparrows and wrens that come to our apple tree. There is no way that the sparrow can force its way into the small door of the wren's house, but it keeps trying. The infuriated wren clings to a branch and fills the air with its fearsome threats, although even its angry music makes a lovely aria.

In the season when the locust trees in our back yard burst into bloom, we watch bumblebees gather such great loads from the blossoms that the big, heavy bees fall to the ground and lie in a drunken stupor. It is the only opportunity given to study a bumblebee up close. Bumblebees are belligerent and sensitive, and have no tolerance for being closely observed.

There are small wonders and minor miracles for a grandfather and grandson to marvel over in our back yard.

There is a sure way of luring us from the river and the Secret Place. Old, empty houses hold a special fascination for us. Some days we drive the station wagon on the side roads around Cooks Mills, looking for old houses to explore. As in all rural areas, the exodus from the farm to the city has left houses standing in bleak commentary on a way of life that used to be. The rich soil is tilled almost to the back door of vacant dwellings and the crops crowd into unused feed lots. Most of the abandoned farm homes are eventually buried by bulldozers and soil spread over the foundations, providing more room for corn and soybeans. Unfortunately, the trend to larger farms and fewer farmers, tilling more and more acreage, has eliminated much of the shelter for wild things. Hedge trees have been replaced by soybeans and the animals desperately seek the few remaining woodlands and meadows.

Roads that would have been impassable in inclement weather in the old days are now smoothed and oiled. We wonder about the people who once lived in the houses and what they would think if they could see the over-sized farm vehicles that pass the old homesteads in all seasons.

With the aid of a little imagination, any old house may take on an air of mystery and speculation. We stand on the sagging porches and speak softly as though someone were standing just out of sight, listening.

There are abandoned wells or cisterns at most old houses. The older ones were usually supplied water by hand-dug wells, enclosed at ground level by a waist high, wooden, hand built curbing. Caution must be used in exploring old houses on the first visit, for the wooden curbings rot. A few wood planks are thrown across the opening and these also rot, forming a real hazard. We are glad the old houses had those hand-dug wells, for all true adventure should be accompanied by an element of danger.

Caution must also be observed inside old houses. The wooden steps leading upstairs creak and pop with our weight.

Our favorite old house was three or four miles north and west of Cooks Mills. It was a two story, weathered frame building, long fallen on hard times. On our first visit I tried not to let Steven see how concerned I was at the condition of the porch and the danger in the steep wooden steps ascending to the second floor.

A colony of bees had swarmed in one of the upstairs corner rooms; we knew we were in greater danger from the bees than from rotted wood or unhappy ghosts. We installed a resident ghost in each old house we explored; the thrill of walking through dead houses is increased by imagining a presence in a closet or behind a door.

We walked through the high-ceilinged rooms, each of us feeling the depression that always accompanies a house that has lost its lived-in feeling. The old houses remember laughing and loving but those memories have given way to the sad strength of loneliness.

Two of the rooms contained nothing but great chunks of fallen plaster and faded wallpaper. We talked of how proud some farm wife must have been of the gaudy flowers running in neat rows up and down the walls of her rooms.

We could look out the shattered windows of the south room and see past the row of river trees. The bell tower seemed to rest in the top branches of the huge maple that stands by the church front steps.

To the east was the Mennonite church and, west, acres of corn and soybeans in rows as exact as the flowers on the wallpaper.

In the northeast upstairs room we found the treasure that set our minds on long thoughts and furnished much discussion at our campfires.

A part of the north wall was marked with pencilled scribblings. There were at least a dozen childishly scrawled arithmetic problems. One simple assignment had been worked three times, each time with a different answer. How that small one must have dreaded school that day. There were long division and multiplication assignments on the dirty, plastered wall. There were two and four line poems of the "roses are red and violets are blue" type. There were names and dates that must have been of great importance.

And then we saw the note, entered as in a diary:

"We buried our little niece today. She looked so pretty in her little blue dress."

The lines were scrawled on the dusty old wall in crude, slanted printing, barely three feet off the floor.

We stood in the shabby upstairs room of the abandoned house, listening to the drone of the bees in the next room and we dreamed a thousand dreams.

The Great Bird

WE THINK IT wise not to concern ourselves with scientific bird watching. We don't know the names of all the birds we see on our hikes. We have them catalogued but they are filed under pleasant memories.

Thor, the hawk, is our special bird. If I visit the Secret Place alone, Steven questions me about Thor. He wants to know if I saw him and if the big hawk was hunting and over which field.

Thor was missing on two consecutive hikes and we thought perhaps he had found a richer hunting ground. The next time I was at Steven's I had news for him: I had seen the hawk as I had crossed the meadow going to the river. I had made the mistake of crossing the meadowland through the center rather than skirting the edge and Thor had flown to other areas before I reached the bottom land. The hawk knew no game would show itself in the wake of my heavy-footed tramping.

We had never seen an eagle outside a zoo. The eagle is not a common sight in our countryside, although a few have been reported.

A dead eagle was found beside a country road in our area a few years ago. One of the newspapers called it a "magnificent specimen" and reported its wing span as measuring several feet. It had been badly mangled by buckshot and left lying in a ditch. We don't know how anyone could get close enough in our flat country to shoot an eagle but why anyone would want to is an even greater mystery. We think there is a penalty for shooting eagles but this is no comfort to the "magnificent specimen" lying in the ditch.

One Saturday morning we were hiking through the north edge of the sassafrass grove and a very large bird rose from a dead limb of a tree a hundred feet to our north. It flew under the lower branches so we caught only a glimpse of it, but the bird was large enough for us to hear even at that distance the rush of air through its feathers. We like to think it was an eagle but it was not a clear sighting, so we will never know.

On the day we did actually see an eagle we were looking for a bird of a different kind.

There had been much publicity about an unidentified bird that had been seen several times in our countryside. It had been reported as a black bird with a red head and a wing span of ten feet or more. It had been classified at various times by various experts as a condor or a turkey buzzard or vulture and there were reports that it had attacked humans.

We were certain the size of the bird had grown with the telling but there was no doubt that something had been seen, and it was larger than anything we had ever observed. We knew we must make an effort to find whatever it was.

The odds were great against our actually tracking down the big bird; the odds were even greater that it would not come to us, so we began driving the station wagon down the country roads in the areas where it had been sighted.

It was a warm Saturday morning and there were many interesting sights on these unfamiliar roads. There was an abandoned house we noted for future exploration. We discovered an old, neatly kept cemetary, with the ever-present pines and evergreens. Close to a seldom travelled road, we found a weathered, unused barn. We could see the knots and the distressed graining from the wagon as we passed and we decided to return and ask the owner for boards for picture framing. An hour passed quickly as we drove.

Suddenly, a shadow floated across the road ahead of our slow-moving station wagon. The shadow was moving from west to east and it was created by an uncommonly large bird.

We stopped the car and stood by the side of the little-used country road, frantically searching the sky with our binoculars.

It was not the big mystery bird but it was an eagle, a very large eagle. We could see its white head and tail. We could not see the fierce glint of freedom that shines in the eyes of all eagles, but we knew it was there. It cast its shadow over us a second time as it glided westward; we felt a sense of loss as we watched it grow small against the pale blue sky.

We travel for fifteen minutes to the river where we bird watch for hours. Most of the birds remain nameless to us, but this does not detract from our enjoyment.

We often watch a little yellow bird we call a wild canary, although someone told us it is a finch. Perhaps there is no such bird as a wild canary but that is what we call it.

This bird's vocabulary consists of one word. It loves that word and uses it on all occasions. Even the bird itself should recognize the absurdity of using that word for territorial claims and trespasss warnings: it endlessly repeats "SWEET...SWEET...SWEET ...SWEET...."

No living thing, not even a little yellow bird, can be expected to be eternally pleasant. All things have an occasional flare of temper, even wild things. We think that some day we may witness an argument over a worm or a nest, and one of the yellow birds will be provoked into saying something stronger than "SWEET."

We know where a big owl lives, but it was several years before we saw it. We had heard its call as we sat at night on the big log beside the campfire. Its voice sounds deeper and richer than those of the other owls hooting at us from the darkness of the river trees. It lives in the maples and oaks shading the river bend near our first Secret Place.

Once, we heard a mob of crows making noises in that grove of trees and were certain they had discovered our friend. Crows are very brave around owls in the daylight; it is the bravery of many against one. They gather in the trees and flap around the limb on which their victim is sitting and make all manner of coarse remarks. The outnumbered owl clutches the tree limb and its head swivels in an almost complete circle. Its huge eyes glare at its tormentors and its beak snaps like a steel trap.

When we heard that gang creating such a raucous commotion, we ran along the river bank and through the brush. The crows heard us coming and left for other parts of the woodland. We did not see the owl, either, although we knew it was somewhere in the masses of leaves. We continued looking for it on each trip to the river, focussing our glasses on possible resting places but we never made a sighting.

One day it came to us.

We were following the path by the river's edge and had not quite reached the bend with the willow trees, when we heard the rustle of air through feathers. As we stood motionless in the path, the big owl lit in a clearing not more than ten feet from us. It stared at us for a moment or two. . .then slowly sailed away.

It was an unforgettable moment.

As we sit by the fire at the campsite in daytime, we see glossy black birds light on the shore on the opposite side of the river. They hop or stroll along the water's edge, carefully investigating each square foot of ground. Each pebble must be pecked at, each leaf turned over, and they always drink at the same shallow pool of water. If we see them the following day, the same pebbles are pecked at, the same leaves turned over and the same pool drunk from.

We don't know what the black bird is called. We don't know the name of the little bird that runs down tree trunks head first. There are many that are nameless, but we know them well.

Many of man's miseries are caused by his pretensions. Life is a kind of continuing act in which we wear different costumes and act out expected roles. Perhaps this is one of our ways of survival.

The creatures in the Secret Place never pretend. We think this may not be merely the result of instinct, but of a divine gift.

When we saw the heron, it was standing on a fallen tree trunk with its head bowed and its wings folded, in the manner of herons. It resembled a little old man with bowed head and hands clasped behind his back in deep thought.

We were able to get quite close before it sensed our presence and flapped away to do its thinking in some more secluded place.

"Do you suppose," said Steven, "it wishes it could soar like a hawk or dart like a wren?"

"If it could think about it," I said, "I doubt if it would compare itself to a hawk. It would take great pride in being a heron." The only time wild things pretend is when they are gifted with the ability to assume disguises to lure their prey or to confuse their predators.

A muskrat is so occupied with being a muskrat and doing muskrat things, it covets no other animal's ways.

It is possible wild things would be shocked if they knew how we compare their ways to the ways of man. If it is true, as some think, that animals have been denied the blessings of love and communication, then neither, perhaps, have they been cursed with jealousy or envy. An argument over a worm or bit of food is not, we think, necessarily covetousness, but an act of hunger.

The Sounds of Hunger

THERE IS ALWAYS tragedy in the Secret Place. Hunger and cold come to the woodlands and the meadow. The river floods and skillfully dug homes are devastated. Snow piles into drifts and dredge ditches freeze and food becomes scarce. There are the hunter and the hunted; the quick and the dead; the fraction of a second's hesitation in flight.

There are a schedule and pattern to the lives of the creatures: like man, wild things build their daily activities around routine and habits. Birds are hatched and the feeding pattern begins. There is a routine of search for food and delivery to the nest. The mother bird will go hungry before she will break the baby bird's feeding pattern.

We have climbed to a nest and snapped our fingers over the heads of the little featherless creatures. All mouths open wide and each little body crowds as closely as possible to our fingers; baby birds are everlastingly hungry.

A dead tree stands near the drift close by our campsite. It has survived the winds and the floods but the years have not been kind to its appearance. It has lost all but two of its limbs and its bark has been gone for many years. At night, the tree shines white in the flickering light of our campfire. Fifteen feet from the ground there is a hole in its trunk the size of a silver dollar.

We were at the campsite one day and as we watched the happenings, we heard a chirping sound coming from the hole in the old dead tree. It was the sound of hungry baby birds.

We moved away, thinking this might encourage the mother to resume her feeding. We watched through our binoculars for a long time but no adult member of the family came to the tree. There was no way to know what had happened but the pattern had been broken.

We returned to the tree and considered ways we might become foster parents. The tree could not be climbed and there was no other close by. We considered bringing a ladder from home.

Even as we talked, we knew we could never keep the little things fed and alive. Despite our feeling for the Place, we can never become a real part of the pattern and we did not want to disrupt it in any way. The Secret Place makes no allowance for adoption. A mother bird will keep her family well fed within sight and sound of another family which is orphaned and starving.

The following day, the sounds were weaker and more desperate.

We stayed away from that place a week.

On our next visit, the cries had ceased.

The Pearl

EACH THING IN the Secret Place displays its own kind of beauty. The beauty may not always be in its plumage or its form but may be in the way it moves or swims or flies; even the things that do not move possess a beauty.

We find a rock in a freshly plowed field and marvel at the way it is veined with varied colors. A chunk of whitened driftwood, ravaged by the waters, displays a unique form of loveliness. Weeds, flourishing for no apparent useful purpose, boast delicate blossoms that we take home for centerpieces. That much-despised, crude-mannered bird, the starling, is feathered with an enviable sheen of color.

Hundreds of mussels make our river their home. There is little beauty to the outside of a mussel. An ugly gray color, it spends its days in the muck of the river bottom. Dozens of mussels are stranded on the mud banks and sand bars during flood times.

Rare beauty is revealed when the shells of the little mollusks are pried apart. The interior glistens snow white, tinged with pink and blue. Sometimes a pearl may be found hidden in the body of the mussel; a pearl is manufactured in a mussel in the same way in which it is manufacturerd in an oyster.

One Saturday afternoon we decided a pearl hunt would be the day's adventures.

Pearl hunting is neither easy nor clean. The mussels must be retrieved from the sand bottoms and the mud banks. Great hunks of clay cling to our hiking boots and our trouser legs become wet and uncomfortable. The shells are hinged with powerful muscles that make it difficult to separate the two halves.

We are told that raccoons pry apart the mussel shells in order to feast on the pure white meat inside. We see many opened mussels lying along the river so this is evidently true. We can hope the raccoons are more efficient at this tasks than we proved to be.

We opened at least twenty-five mussels that afternoon and found no pearls. It was a warm day and we perspired as we plodded in the mud and strained at the shells. Our boots were heavy with river mud and our hands were slippery with it.

We decided to leave the mussels to the river and the raccoons and began to walk north along the bank, winding our way around the debris of the recent flood. The wood was damp and the ground saturated with water; we knew it would be difficult to build a fire. As we walked the river path, we saw the biggest mussel of the day lying on a newly formed plateau of mud. This large specimen was half submerged in the mire. Steven's boots sank in six inches of mud and water as he trudged out for the prize and wrestled it from the mud.

When we had pried open the shells we ran our fingers along the bulk of the body but found no pearl. So I left Steven with the mussel and started walking toward the maple grove at the foot of the hill.

Suddenly, I heard him call and turned to see him running through the underbrush, cupped hands outstretched. Words were unnecessary. He had found a pearl in that last big mussel.

Although small, it was the most perfect pearl I had ever seen. It was a delicately tinted off-white and so perfectly round that when we placed it on a mirror it rolled without our touching it. A jeweller told us it was one of the finest fresh water pearls he had ever had in his shop and appraised it at six dollars. Six dollars is not a great amount of money but a number of six dollar pearls strung together would be a necklace of some value.

The value of the pearl lay not in appraisals but in the finding.

The value of my day is measured by the memory of the boy running through the woods with the pearl cupped in his outstretched hands, and a look of joy on his face.

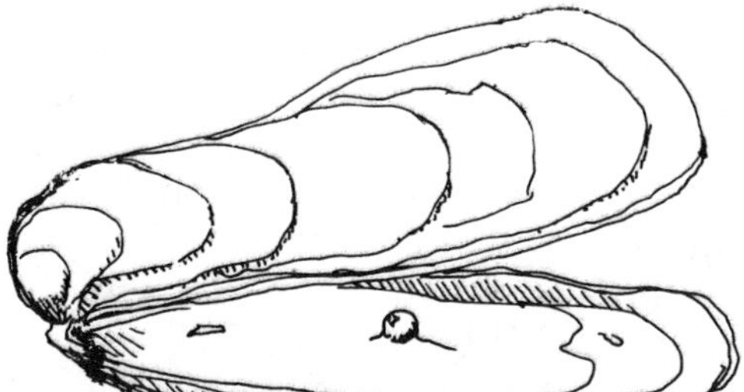

Sounds in the Night

AFTER YEARS OF absence, the deer have returned to our countryside in such numbers they are becoming a nuisance to farmers. They are said to break down fences and to forage in the crops. They are stalked and hunted with guns and with bows and arrows but their numbers are increasing, even in this hostile world. We have seen them on the crest of our hill as we sit at breakfast. The hilltop and the sassafrass grove can be plainly seen from our kitchen window, so that sometimes Grandma will look out and see us returning from a hike. If our bodies are bent against the wind tearing at our jackets and our faces are flushed with cold, she will rush to warm two cups of hot chocolate.

We have studied the imprint of deer hooves in soft ground and one night we heard one bounding through the dried leaves in the woods as we came home from a hike.

We know deer are fond of salt and will travel great distances to salt-baited areas. It is illegal, as it should be, for hunters to bait deer, but our goal was not to hunt but to observe.

We devised a simple plan. I was to carry salt to the river a day or two before a hike and scatter it beneath the river trees. We hoped the deer would discover their favorite snack.

Late one cold Thursday afternoon, I took my bag of salt down the lane and over the hill to the river and placed its contents in neat piles near the campsite. The brittle twigs crackled underfoot and the woods were as quiet as church on Monday morning.

I scattered enough salt to lure many deer. If all the salt were consumed, we would observe a herd of very thirsty deer.

I sat alone and watched the cold water flow awhile. It was getting late and darkness comes quickly under the trees at the river's edge so I went back through the meadow and up the hill into the sunshine.

Two nights later, we ate an early dinner and waited impatiently for the dark.

We had put on our insulated underwear and heavy clothing and stocking caps and our lined hiking boots, for the hilltop is cold on a windy winter night.

Our plan was to carry flashlights but not use them until we arrived at the baiting place. Then we would flash our lights and catch the deer licking at our salt.

We moved cautiously down the lane. It is difficult to travel without light and we had not realized the lane held so many chuckholes and ridged ruts. We picked our way along with our staffs as we walked in the darkness.

The appearance of the Secret Place changes dramatically at night. Familiar stumps and trees assume menacing shapes. We feel alien, for the real world is farther from the make believe one. Sounds on the river are not as easily recognized as in the daylight.

A dog barks in the village and is answered by another. In the night it is easy to visualize this as a call for the gathering of the wild pack. The polkberry bush that shelters quail takes on the shape of Big Foot, his long arms dangling almost to the ground as he stands and waits for us. A glint of light reflects on the metal of the old tractor and becomes two bright, staring eyes, questioning our right to be on the hillside at a time that belongs to the night creatures.

We knew the deer were not troubling themselves over shadow shapes and imagined creatures and even now might be licking at the salt we had provided, so we pressed on.

We reached the river and began to walk very slowly, heels down first to make the least noise. We felt for the bushes ahead of us. Truthfully, a large man and a growing boy do not move through the woods at night as silently as they would wish, and Steven whispered that a deer would have to be either deaf or crazy not to hear us coming through the underbrush. Finally, we were at the baited area, prepared to flash our lights.

Suddenly we heard the sharp crack of a large limb, broken by something in full flight. An unexpected sound is most startling on a still, dark night. We stopped and listened.

As we waited and listened, something coughed in the shadows. It was a loud cough: it could have been a deer or it could have been anything. A cough is not a frightening sound unless it is heard under trees by the river on a dark night and is accompanied by the crack of a breaking limb.

We wish we could tell how we flashed our lights and ran toward the baited area and saw a herd of deer escaping in the dark.

The truth is, we flashed our lights and walked rapidly in the opposite direction. Grandma was surprised at the brevity of our adventure but assured us it was commonsense and not cowardice that moved us to leave the sounds and come home.

However, it is unnerving to feel you may have been frightened from your special world by a coughing deer.

Scavenging and Treasure Hunting

PROFESSIONAL BEACHCOMBERS WOULD not be excited by the objects we scavenge from the river bank. We find no chambered shells, exotic fish or artifacts from far off places. However, we do discover things that cause us to wonder where they came from and how they arrived at the Secret Place.

Some finds are easily understood. The red jon boat with the stoved in side that floated for months in the big log jam south of the cabin had obviously been swept from its mooring place upstream, for the frayed anchoring rope still dangled from the bow. Flood waters must have whirled the boat with the currents until it snagged itself on the drift. The space between the seats collected rain water and made an efficient and convenient holding tank for our fish catches.

It was a little more difficult to explain the piece of luggage that arrived with the boat. A black metal suitcase, complete with compartments and buckled straps, sat on the floor between the middle and front seat. We have never heard of a fisherman packing a suitcase to ride the river in a jon boat.

Once, we found a red fishing tackle box lying near the water's edge. It was like new and had been carefully cleaned. Each compartment had been washed and wiped until it was spotless. In one of the little dividers there were thirteen new fish hooks, wrapped in toilet paper. There was no trace of the gear that normally clutters a fishing tackle box. The sinkers, bobbers, leaders, lures, all were gone, leaving just thirteen new hooks, taken from their package, wrapped in toilet paper and discarded along with the box.

Our route to the Secret Place normally follows a set pattern. We walk down the hill to the tractor, climb the barbed wire fence, skirt the edges of the briar patch, and walk in under the crabapple trees. We climb a second fence, east of the Amishman's horse pasture, wind our way through a grove of bottomland and sapling trees and arrive at the river path leading to the campsite, a quarter mile north.

We walk slowly, allowing sufficient time to observe and interpret what we see. We see the bank poles left overnight by Cooks Mills fishermen. There will often be a channel catfish struggling on one line, the slim sapling bending with the weight of the fish until the tip of the homemade pole touches the water. The bank pole whips in a frenzy and the water eddies as the cat fights for its life. If the fisherman does not retrieve his catch quickly enough, a snake or turtle will have a grand feast off the helpless fish.

We travel this route so frequently and so slowly that anything out of place or out of the ordinary attracts our immediate attention.

One morning we had hiked a few feet north on the river path when we saw something lying ahead in the middle of the well-worn trail. We had been this way the night before and had not seen anything unusual.

Lying directly in the path was a rusted pulley, the kind used by local farmers to hoist bales of hay or straw into their barn lofts. Lying next to the pulley was a pickaxe head. They were strange companions to be abandoned together on a remote river bank, for they bore no relevance to each other. The pulley weighed at least ten pounds and the pickaxe head, five or six. Each, though rusted, was in good condition and neither could have floated downstream.

Someone carried those two heavy objects to the river during the night and left them lying in the trail. Why?

At flood times, when the currents run wild and eddy around half-submerged log jams, we see plastic bleach bottles bobbing in the froth. Occasionally, the bleach bottles carry lines and hooks. Someone upstream has been jug fishing and the river has swiped his gear.

Long lengths of trout-fishing line with vicious-looking big black hooks are a common find, as are bobbers and floats.

Once we found a brand new baseball bat floating at the water's edge. We wondered if someone had thrown it into the river in a fit of pique and vowed never to play again. Fun games become so serious with some people.

We build chilling scenarios around the possibility

of a human body floating downstream, with hand outflung in a mute cry for help. Sitting at night by the campfire with the sounds of the flood waters near by, we conjure visions of what may be turning and twisting in the currents close to us.

We were enroute to the cabin one chilly day. We had decided to build a fire in a ravine we knew lay just south of the cabin. Sheltered by steep banks on the west and protected from the north winds by trees along the river bend, the gully would be an ideal place to warm our feet and observe the river happenings, north and south.

As we neared the ravine, we saw four white, circular objects shining in the dead leaves and weeds. There had been nothing visible at that spot on our last trip so we quickened our pace to see what could have been cast away in such a conspicuous place.

We found four white dinner plates of striking appearance. They had been arranged as though dinner were being set for four. Silverware was lacking but it appeared as if someone had set places for a river picnic in this unlikely place and in such unlikely weather.

The china was faultless and each carried a print of a Dickensian character smoking a long stemmed pipe as he stood near a table laden with food. A dog lay at his feet, begging for scraps. The name of an English firm was imprinted on the backs of the plates.

We built our fire and warmed our feet and wondered at what series of circumstances caused the fine china to be set so neatly in a ravine on the banks of the Okaw.

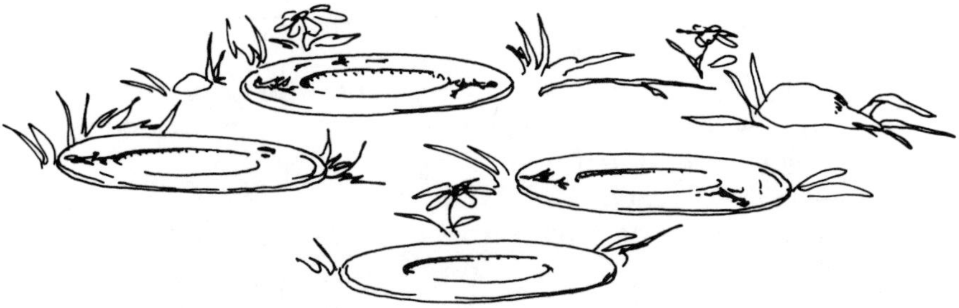

Reading Signs

WE OFTEN WISH we could "read signs" in the manner of the grizzled old trappers and Indian scouts in Western movies. Each crushed weed or snapped twig tells its tale to the tracker's keen eye. He determines if a trail is "hot" or "cold." He calculates whether one person or two is riding a horse. He is infallible.

We make a study of the trails in the Secret Place and are able, in an amateurish way, to interpret some of the triumphs and tragedies in the everyday life of the wild things. Sign reading is an exacting science and we have taught ourselves only enough to make us long to know more.

We find bluejay feathers scattered along the edge of a grassy ditch. The tips of the feathers are blood-flecked and we speculate whether this signifies a territorial fight with another jay or if a precious fraction of time had been lost, allowing a fox to spring.

We follow a rabbit's tracks. The prints are evenly spaced for a while as though the rabbit was going about its daily rabbit routine but, suddenly, the tracks are farther apart, measured in feet rather than inches and they zig-zag. The rabbit has been running fast, taking great leaps. From the right-hand side, a dog's tracks join those of the rabbit and each set of prints leads towards a barbed wire fence and a briar patch. The rabbit had made its habitual move, a tactic employed by its tribe for centuries. We run to the other side of the briar patch as fast as the snow drifts will allow us. The tracks separate. The rabbit ran south and we can see the dog headed north in a long circle, then swung back to the rabbit's trail.

We smile at each other. The dog has become confused. In the Secret Place, life or death hinges on such things. The rabbit has done it again. It has survived.

After a snow or rain, the banks of the Okaw bear hundreds of tracks. There are so many raccoon tracks we wonder if a lot of 'coons travel a little, or a few 'coons travel a lot. Mixed with the raccoon tracks may be those of a running dog. Perhaps another chase and another tragedy, although dogs seldom are winners in a contest with raccoons, unless assisted by hunters and guns.

There are many pencil-thin claw marks on the bank, where birds have come to drink. Sometimes we see a few feathers and drops of blood. This tells us that for some the night has not been gentle.

WE TRAVEL LIGHT on our journeys into the Secret Place. Our gear consists of staffs, a pair of binoculars, flash lights for night hikes, and sometimes a drawing pad and pencil.

Over the years, Steven has accumulated a collection of plastic and rubber figurines. I was allowed to enter the make-believe world in which those characters lived. King Arthur, General Custer, the Ringo Kid and dozens of foot soldiers and horsemen—each served his time in great land and sea battles.

We never took the collection to the river: it was stored away for rainy days. It would have been an extra load to carry, and there was plenty to see and do in the Secret Place. The little figures never seemed to be a real part of our special world.

As we grew older we spent less time with the little people and our walks to the river became more studied. Steven began to read and discuss Thoreau. It was the second time around for me; I enjoyed the work of that gentle philospher. *Walden* and the other books became even more meaningful shared with a fellow reader.

The boxes in which lay our splendid fighting men, and their weapons and horses, gathered dust. Occasionally we would open them and discuss past deeds. Some soldiers were beginning to show the passage of time; an arm or a leg would be missing. A shoe would be gone from a foot and sometimes the foot itself would no longer be attached to the body.

One little man in particular, a fierce Viking, had run more than his share of gauntlets. His costume, with horned helmet and wrap-around leggings, was tattered and torn and his bristling moustache was minus many bristles. His face was scarred and his sword arm was gone from his body.

It seemed fitting we should dispatch him to Valhalla in the manner of all Norsemen, by way of a funeral pyre, and there was no better setting for a Viking Funeral than the world of the Secret Place.

As we walked to the Secret Place, bearing our fallen comrade, I remembered that Steven had once said that if anything ever happened to him, "like a car wreck, or something," I should walk along the river and feel sure he was walking with me. Truthfully, this makes as much sense as some of the promises spoken at real life funerals.

We reached the river, near the campsite, and prepared our Viking for his entry to Valhalla. We had found his sword arm and we placed it near his battered body, for surely when he reached the great halls and was greeted by his fellow rovers, his good right arm would once again be in fighting position, else it would not be Valhalla. His helmet had lost one of its horns but Vikings were never much concerned with appearances.

We found a piece of bark that was shaped, more or less, like a ship. We placed our fighting man on this makeshift boat and piled dried grass and twigs around his body.

The river was in a gentle mood and the currents flowed slowly. We placed the crude craft and its burden at the waters' edge, then lit our pyre.

The flames crackled and blazed around our little hero as we shoved his boat into the river and we could see his features begin to melt and his legs curl back under his body. No Viking ever had a grander funeral than our little friend, sailing down the Okaw, with the flames leaping around him.

Alas, the noble warrior floated only a few feet down stream before his boat snagged on a partially submerged log. We spent much time looking for a long pole with a forked end with which we could pull the boat and its passenger ashore in order to resume the services.

The little fighting man was badly burned but not entirely consumed although the grasses and twigs had been reduced to a blackened mass. We tenderly rearranged the charred body and covered it once again with dry material but this time we placed the Viking in a sitting position. It seemed more appropriate.

We lit the grasses a second time and pushed the boat far out into the current. The warrior looked ridiculously like a badly burned, indignant little man, sitting on a bed roll, watching the river shore from his boat. His stern features had sagged and the helmet he once wore so proudly had melted into a plastic pancake and had fallen over his brow.

We ran along the river shore throwing chunks of clay and huge sticks in the water so that the waves from our projectiles would keep his boat in midstream.

By this time, even the most hardened Viking would have tired of such disorganized services and would have gone sailing off somewhere to conquer something. We thought the custom of burning the funeral pyre would have disappeared long before it did if all Viking families had experienced such problems in disposing of their loved ones.

A day or two later, Steven was exploring downstream from where we had abandoned our friend and he discovered the Viking, still sitting upright in his funeral craft with the ashes around him. He was caught in a log jam and the boat and the Viking and the ashes swayed back and forth with the current.

It seemed an ignominious end for our little warrior from the northlands.

Outdoor Cooking

A HIKE UP and down the hill, across the meadow and along the river stimulates a hearty appetite, but the meals were plentiful and tasty at home. Time spent in preparing lunches would mean less time for observing.

One Saturday morning, we agreed to return to the ways of those who travelled the river in past days and prepare our own meals, from scratch. We chose our menu carefully, trying to simulate a menu of the early settlers.

We decided a couple of steaks would serve as a fitting substitute for chunks of bear meat or venison. However, our forefathers were frugal folks so on second thought, we chose hamburger rather than steaks, which they would have done, had they the choice.

We were concerned about taking fresh bakery bread, rather than sour dough, but we rationalized that even the most independent pioneers would have shopped in a settlement store, if they could. It seemed a minor flaw that our bread was pre-sliced.

We planned on preparing eggs and potatoes by rolling them in river bottom mud and laying them to bake in the coals of our fire.

We knew the settlers used salt and pepper so we added these staples to our growing list of supplies. Mustard and catsup seemed logical additions and took up little room in an already bulging pack.

Potatoes or eggs rolled in mud hold little attraction for man ancient or modern, so we decided to enclose sliced potatoes in foil and let them fry over a flame. We would need a grill but we rationalized, once again, that if the earlier people had owned a grill, they would have used it. We felt they would have enjoyed more sophisticated dining if it had been possible.

We could imagine their stopping off at any grocery or variety store that might be handy on their western trek. They would be wearing their bib overalls and floppy hats and knee-high boots and they would shop for some of the niceties, such as napkins and toothpicks. In line with this thinking, we took some cookies and cold pop.

We started to the river, heavily burdened with our supplies and gear. We rested many times on the way, assuring each other our frequent stops were made in order for us to observe the happenings.

Arriving at the campsite, we began to build our cooking fire, which differs from the roaring blaze we usually stoke for sitting and talking purposes. The gods of the winds were against us that day and we spent a great deal of time striking matches and puffing at the embers in an effort to maintain the proper sized fire.

After the flames were going to our satisfaction, we placed our grill on some rocks we had picked up along the river's edge and had hauled back to circle the fire bed.

We carefully placed our potatoes and our four huge hamburgers on the grill. Gray ashes flew up and settled on the meat when we poked the red coals.

We sat on a log and watched and waited. The hamburgers sizzled as grease dropped on the hot coals and we could hear frying noises coming from inside the foil wrapping.

We were hungry although we had eaten breakfast scarcely three hours before. The noises and the aroma helped build our anticipation. We wondered how many wild things were watching from their hiding places. Perhaps they, too, loved the smell of cooking food.

Neither of us knew the proper cooking time for either potatoes or hamburger. We checked our watches freqently but the time passed ever so slowly and the meat showed no signs of being cooked. Thinking that ersatz bear meat would most certainly be well done on one side, we attempted to turn the patties but two of them slid across our grill and on to the ground. Our potatoes rolled off, also, although they were protected by the foil.

We thought it would be a good idea to toast our bread but our plans went awry and we settled for two blackened slabs, hardly recognizable as bread.

At last, we decided we should eat and we sat at our fire and crunched at our burned bread and raw potatoes and nibbled our half done hamburger. Our cold pop had turned warm and flat.

We told each other many times how exciting it was to relive the past and agreed that food always tastes better in the open air. We never admitted defeat, but we each ate a huge meal at home that evening.

We never see a movie of the olden days that we do not feel a grudging respect for those aproned ladies who set such satisfying tables in the face of such adversities.

Tell us, people from our past, did you never tire? Were there not times when you cursed the wet wood and the east wind and the choking smoke of your campfires? Were your steaks grilled to order with some medium and some medium well or did you give thanks you were able to cook them in any style at all? Did your fires always start with the first strike of the flint? How could you travel far in your day's march if your cooking time was as prolonged as ours?

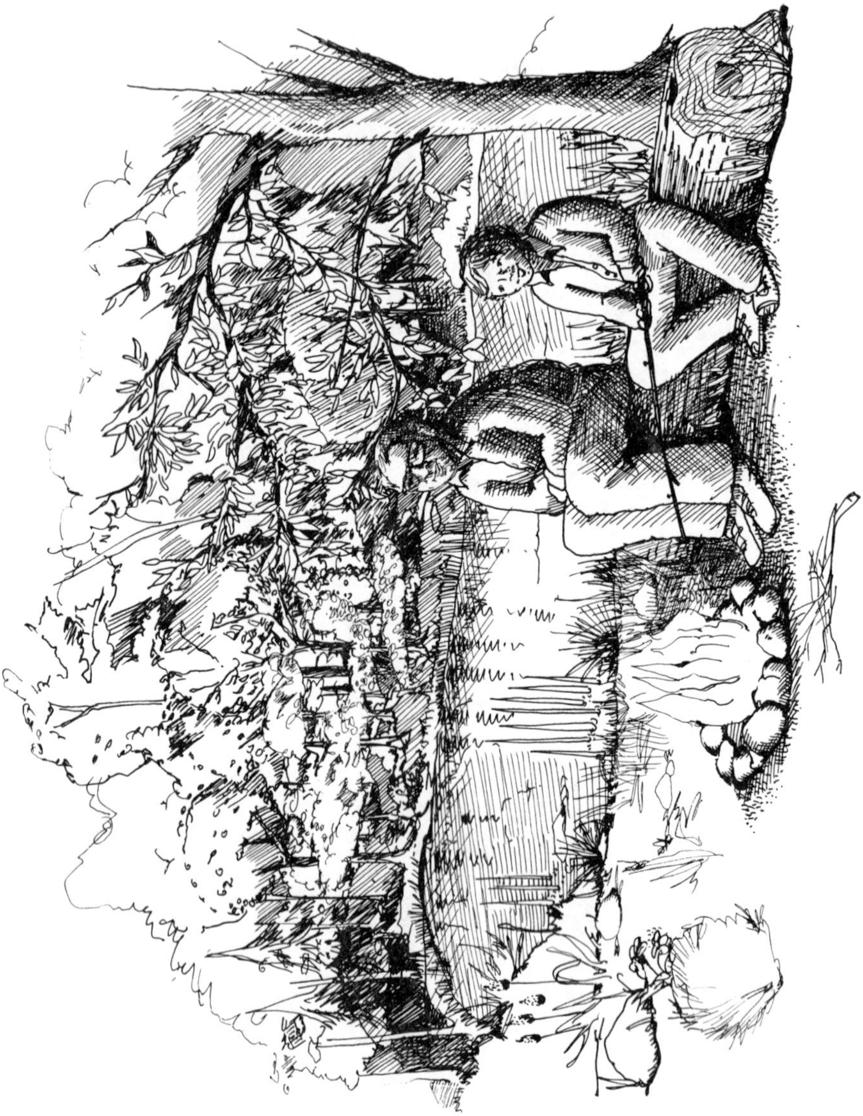

We Build a Hogan

STEVEN EXPRESSES SOME disappointment at my lack of enthusiasm for roughing it along the river. He builds glowing word pictures of the joys of night camping: sitting by the campfire until late hours, then lying in our bedrolls under the stars, listening to the river and to the sounds of the night creatures.

I, personally, am not convinced that the Indians who lived along the Okaw so many years ago were all that enthusiastic over the rough life they lived. Surely not all of them looked forward to sacking out on the uneven, rock-strewn ground. There must have been a few who spent sleepless nights, twisting and turning, trying to find a smooth place and wondering what was moving in the bushes in the dark. It is reasonable to assume no tribe is one hundred percent valiant.

When the tribe moved to a new hunting ground, the first item on the agenda was to build wigwams or hogans. Some of these were quite elaborate, with space for family heirlooms and keepsakes and the walls were decorated with painted symbols. These structures would be built with cleverly placed holes at the top to allow campfire smoke to escape. There would be heaps of animals skins on which to sleep and a small door in front, facing south. Each family could crawl into its hogan with its medicine bags and pow wow pipes and tell family stories and reminisce. Not much privacy but warm and comfortable.

We made plans to build a hogan patterned after an illustration in a back-to-nature handbook. We chose our location in mid-summer but it was a month into winter before we began construction.

The grove of maples at the foot of the hill was to be the site of our hogan. Flood waters carry tree limbs and small logs and leave them lying at the edge of this patch of woods and the maples' lower limbs are garlanded with dried grasses and weeds as further evidence of the high water mark. The grove itself is surprisingly free of debris and underbrush and offers a clearing that is the proper size for hogan building.

There was an invigorating chill in the air that morning as we walked down the hill and into the meadow. By the time we had staked our site and begun choosing logs for the framework, the wind had gathered force and was flowing over the crest of the hill and down its slope with an intensity that chilled our finger tips as we worked. The wind carried a mist with it that became cheek-stinging pellets of ice. Most of the trees were small and afforded little protection. We stamped our feet and clapped our hands for warmth, as we had decided to deny ourselves the luxury of a fire until it could be built inside our completed hogan.

We began by standing ten foot logs on end, leaning against each other in the shape of a cone. Our dwelling soon began to take shape and we felt a sort of pride, although we were wet and uncomfortable. After we placed each log, we would step back and admire our work.

Our next step was to encircle the framework with smaller branches and dried leaves. Around and around we went with our branches, covering all but a small hole on the south side, which was to serve as our door. We had changed our minds about building a fire in that huge mass of dried leaves and limbs but we left a hole in the top for the sake of authenticity.

We spent much of our time crawling in and out of our little door and the knees of our trousers became soggy and chilly from the cold, wet ground. We pretended our trips inside were for the purpose of checking the interior of our hogan but, truthfully, it was the only way to escape the driving wind and snow. We finally cast away all pretense and huddled inside our half built wigwam, peering out the little door at the swirling snow.

Our conversation turned to the fireplace and the hot chocolate waiting at home. The boughs and leaves we had hauled and piled on the framework gave little protection from the elements and the hole in the roof was large enough to allow discomforting seepage of snow and cold rain.

It was one of the few times we were defeated by the Secret Place. The fox and the squirrels were in their dens and the other wild things were sheltered as they were supposed to be in this angry weather. Perhaps the wind and the snow were a respite in the battle for survival for if there were no friends afoot, neither were there enemies.

We did not belong in the Place on this day. The world that had given us so many hours of sunlight and warm waters had turned hostile and bitter. The trees we had once seen covered with hundreds of Monarch butterflies on their annual pilgrimage now gathered ice crystals on their bony fingers. The Place was letting us know that life on the river could be harsh and something to be endured rather than enjoyed.

Slowly, angling our bodies against the wind, and covering our faces with our hands, we began the climb up the hill. The path had never seemed so long. The lane had become a quarter mile passageway with east and west windows opened to the sleet and snow.

It was a never to be forgotten time. The Place had sent us home with a memory and we would not trade that memory for recollections of warmer days and sunnier skys.

We talked of defeat. We tend to remember only the successes of those whom we admire. Surely not all Indians chipped perfect arrowheads and built rain-proof hogans. There must have been some whose ineptitude was the talk of the tribe and there may even have been some who hired their arrows chipped and their hogans built. It is not too ridiculous to think there could have been Indian contractors and subcontractors.

We returned to the grove the following week. There had been a freeze, then a thaw, then another freeze. The river had pushed its way over the ice and snow and into our clearing.

The mud stopped us a few feet from our hogan but we could see it had stood against the flood and enough remained to mark it as a man-made structure. We felt pride in what we had done and vowed that at another time and with more lenient weather we would return and build a hogan that would be the envy of all the red ghosts watching us from behind the trees.

These Are Not Our Favorite Things

NOT ALL OUR encounters in the Secret Place are pleasant ones. We have become acquainted with the discomfort of briars and tickle grass. Spanish needles cling to our pants legs and our socks and the hard little seeds must be removed one at a time. The leaves on low branches brush our faces as we walk down the river path, and gnats swarm around us in untold numbers. Smoke from our campfires follows us as we circle around the blaze, our eyes tear-filled. We have been dive bombed by mosquitoes and bumblebees make threatening gestures. We must be watchful for poison ivy and poison oak. We have met each of these discomforts in its own time and place. Each is a part of the Secret Place.

Mud is one of the greater handicaps to the enjoyment of the Secret Place. It clings to our hiking boots after a rain or thaw and must be scraped off with our knife blades and scrubbed at with clumps of leaves or weeds. It becomes an especially tiring chore to carry half dried logs to our campfire, while tracking through slippery mud. It is difficult to sit at our observation points along the river when the ground carries a layer of mud and the logs are wet from recent rains.

However, even mud is blessed with good features. It presents us with an easily read journal of the night's happenings along the river bank. In one area we may see the tracks of a raccoon pressed into the mud as the creatures came to drink during the night hours. We find the prints of a dog's paws close by those of the 'coon's; perhaps the raccoon has paid dearly for its drink. We find the tracks of 'posssums, tails dragging.

The 'possum is an untidy creature, caring little for looks and it sleeps most of the day.

Bird tracks of all sizes cross and recross the mud banks.

We have never noticed a sign showing where a wild thing has slipped or floundered in the mud, as we so often do. We wonder if there are no raccoons or 'possums that dread walking by the river side for fear they may slide into the water. We must cling to small trees and sturdy bushes as we travel on sloping ground. How did the animals learn to mudwalk so much more efficiently than we?

The Secret Place undergoes a change with each rain. New beauty is added. Green grass is resurrected from its brown and dried death. Log jams and drifts are rearranged. New sand bars are formed, then erased. Until the river recedes, we fish for carp and catfish over the flood-covered trails and river paths.

We understand the rain and the life it brings and the death that comes without it. However, the rain creates problems on our hikes.

We stand in our backyard and watch the dark gray clouds roll toward us and assure one another the storm is going around and that the skies will soon be clear. The lightning leaps from cloud to cloud and hammers the earth and we remember the danger of being caught under tall trees in a storm. We decide to wait out the rain and if we are fortunate, the shower doesn't last long and we start for the river, knowing full well the discomforts we will experience.

The wet weeds soak our trouser legs long before we reach the first observation point. Our socks are wet and they bunch up under the soles of our feet. Each touch of a clump of wet leaves brings a cold shower.

The river will not rise for a few hours but the fish sense it has rained and they will be coming to the banks and the mouths of the inlets to feed. They feast on the bugs and worms washed down from the fields and weeds along the river. It would be a very good time to go fishing.

There is no way to escape the wet. Trees and bushes are saturated. The river bank is slippery and treacherous and we clutch at sapling trees as we hike.

But we know the moment of magic will come, the happening that is the reason for this trip.

The clouds disintegrate and blue sky replaces gray. Warm sunlight filters through the leaves and patterns the water. A bird sits in a close-by tree and sings a territorial song. The sun is shining and life begins again.

It is a good place to be and a good time to be there.

A Special Dislike

WE HAVE A special dislike for ticks. At certain times of the year we must inspect ourselves after each hike to make certain we are not hosting the persistent nuisances. Steven seldom complains of the discomforts we experience on our journeys but he carries a deep hatred of ticks.

The big, black dog is also a non-complainer. We have seen him flounder through the ice and fall into cold river water. Except for a pained yelp at first contact, he shows nothing but enthusiasm as he paddles toward us as though swimming in freezing water were a part of his daily routine.

Sometimes when he meets us, we see the bloody gashes on his face and the freshly ripped ears and know they are the marks of a recent battle. With those big teeth and long, hard nails, he would be a formidable adversary.

He displays his usual joy of living, paying little attention to his wounds. We almost expect him to shuffle his big feet and say, "Aw shucks, it ain't nothing."

However, ticks drive him into a frenzy of complaints. He tears at his hide as though he were about to devour himself. Ticks pose a unique problem for the dog family, for they will often attach themselves to places unreachable by tooth or claw and the dog is in torment until we pull the ticks for him.

Once, we discovered what we thought would be a happy addition to our Secret Place.

An abandoned road runs close by the old cemetery and goes one quarter mile south to a clear little stream. It passes under water and re-emerges to wander through a wooded area and past a cow pasture. This was a much used thoroughfare in the old days but misuse and neglect have rendered it impassable. Faint tracks are still visible where the buggies and wagons bumped along on their way to Cooks Mills but the midway is choked with waist high weeds.

There was formerly a one room school on the west side of the road. Since the school was painted a bright red, it was known locally as "Little Red." We assume there was a "Big Red" somewhere in the country side.

Years ago an iron bridge spanned the little stream but the bridge has long since toppled to one side and only the foundation stone and parts of the iron railing remain. The wooden flooring planks have rotted away or been washed downstream in times of flood.

The stream itself is about two feet deep, ten feet wide and gifted with the clearest water we have seen on any of our hikes. Each grain of the white sand that layers the bottom of the brook is clearly visible. Rocks and pebbles, worn smooth by years of washing, are strewn in the channel.

There are dozens of crawdaddies darting backward on the bottom of the stream, stirring little white sand storms in the water. Swarms of top water minnows swim in erratic bursts of speed, just under the surface. Minnows live a life of perpetual panic and swim frantically away at the slightest movement or if just a shadow crosses their territory.

Steven fashioned a catching bucket from an old can we found under a nearby tree and used it to scoop out minnows and baby crawfish. After a few minutes of study, we would place the struggling creatures back into the water. Each would move swiftly about as though trying to avoid a second catastrophe, then settle down to routine, the experience apparently forgotten.

We pulled off our shoes and socks and waded until we saw we were stirring up great clouds of sand and frightening minnows and crawdaddies, making observation impossible.

We sat on the gently sloping bank and let the sun dry our feet as we talked of our new found observation place and how we would make this a regular stopping place on our hikes.

Steven rolled his pants leg a few inches higher, in preparation for further wading and exploration and discovered a tick had buried itself under the skin. Then we found another and another.

We had waded through the clumps of weeds smothering the gravel of the road bed in order to reach this idyllic spot and we knew the ticks were waiting for us in those weeds.

We forced ourselves to return through that weed patch, walking swiftly and not stopping until we had arrived at a place where the ruts had survived the assault of the weeds.

We remember the crawdaddies and the minnows and the soft, white sand, but we have never returned.

The Swarm

ONE SATURDAY AFTERNOON, we explored the place where the one room school, "Little Red," once stood. All that remains is the grove of oak and hickory trees that once sheltered the playground. We talked of the generations of children that had played under those trees at recess time. We thought of how cold that one room must have been with only a potbellied stove to battle the prairie winds. The "gymnasium" consisted of two basketball backboards at either end of a cinder court, packed hard by years of pounding bare feet. Boys' and girls' rest rooms were wooden shacks at opposite ends of the school yard. It was not necessary to impose a dress code since no student had much of a wardrobe. The usual dress was bibbed overalls and blue shirts for the boys and long dresses for the girls.

We walked farther south along the old road, checking the ditches and fence rows for rabbit or quail.

We noticed an old hot water tank lying by the roadside. We could identify it by the faucets and receiving pipes but the tank itself was covered with a moving, restless mass of insects. Not an inch of metal was left uncovered and as we moved closer, we heard the buzz of thousands of bees. They were swarming on the tank and it looked as though all the bees in all the meadows in the Secret Place had congregated at that spot.

The bees were constantly moving, shifting positions, crawling from one place to another, humming like a multitude of tiny motors. Occasionally one would rise a few inches into the air, then drop back into the seething mass.

We watched awhile, speculating on the furious activity and why such an unlikely swarming place was chosen.

There is a remarkable kind of concentration exhibited by all forms of life: a spider crawling across the path ahead of us seems to know exactly where it is going and what it will do when it gets there. All its willpower is directed toward going and being. Its attention may be momentarily distracted by an obstruction in its path, but as soon as the coast is clear, it will resume its concentrated journey. Only ants become confused about the purpose of their journeys.

We knew we were in little danger as long as we remained a respectful distance from the swarm, although they were so intent on their activites they would probably not have noticed us.

We retreated to an even safer distance and began pitching chunks of dirt at the tank and its blanket of bees. We did not throw into the swarm itself, but peppered the sides of the tank with pieces of dirt. The moving would cease for a fraction of a second, then positions would shift with the precision of a well trained team. A few bees rose to circle above the tank then drop back into the main body to move and buzz.

We stood there a long time, watching and wondering and, maybe, a little uneasy. And then a strange and wonderful thing happened. A flight of perhaps five or six bees flew toward us, while the rest of the swarm buzzed away, unconcerned.

We could see them and we could hear them but we didn't take time to count them. We ran. We ran past the place where "Little Red" once stood, as the bees harassed and dove at us repeatedly.

Steven had yanked off his floppy "frontiersman's" hat and was waving it over his head in frantic circles as he ran, bent over at the waist, in hopes of presenting a smaller target. I was hatless so I wig-wagged my handkerchief as I ran in hopes they would strike it, rather than me. We were shouting words of encouragement to each other as we ran, laughing at our undignified retreat.

The bees roughly escorted us to the corner where thee two roads meet, then returned to their swarm.

We don't know if our attackers were chosen to disperse eavesdroppers by the other bees or if they were a few who had decided that enough is enough: a self-respecting bee can tolerate only so much dirt-throwing and then must rise in righteous wrath.

We went back the next day and they were gone.

The Hoax

WE MARVEL AT how archaelogists are capable of drawing volumes of information from a very small book. Chipped bits of flint at the remains of ancient campfires, stripes of paint slashing across the walls of caves, crude figures laboriously carved into the side of a rock—each of these tells a story to the trained watcher.

Our Secret Place was not always surrounded by rich farm lands traversed by well-travelled roads. Once there was a swamp, and head-high prairie grass; ancient tribes flourished and disappeared. A glacier covered our Place during the last Ice Age, although geologists say it halted its crushing advance a few miles south of our river.

Farmers in our area unearth arrowheads and stone axes during spring plowing. Burial grounds have been uncovered. Some of the neighbors have collections of artifacts whose variety and quality could rival that of any museum.

Many of the rocks we find lying in the fields as we hike bear the marks of modern discs and plows, but we think some are scarred by the great glacier itself. Sometimes we dig beneath the rich top soil with our staffs and pry out large stones and we think of how we have brought to light objects that may be millions of years old, hidden from man for who knows how long.

Once, we were studying such a rock and speculating about its past. It was of porous sandstone material and about the size of a man's head. One side was flattened and smooth.

Steven began idly scratching at the flattened side with his knife blade and in a few moments, I could see the form of a little stick man, like a child's drawing. The little man was running, his head bent forward and his arms and legs flailing. Over the scratched circle which was the little man's head, Steven carved another, larger circle, representing the sun. Rays from the sun shone down on the little man as he ran. It took only a little more time and effort to add a cloud and a series of scratches that could be symbols. Steven's work became more ambitious and he added arrows flying through the air and a wigwam.

All these were engraved as deeply as possible and when he had finished, he had what appeared to be an artifact from a lost civilization. We read it as the story of an Indian who had gone hunting on a warm day and had encountered a hostile neighbor, from whom he was fleeing to the safety of his wigwam.

We left the rock half hidden in the weeds along a fence row and as we walked home, we built scenarios around the future discovery of our "ancient artifact." Maybe some other grandson and grandfather would thrill at the find, and our rock would be known as "The Cooks Mills Stone" and would be studied with much gravity and many consultations.

Hibernation

WE DO NOT trouble ourselves with explanations of the wonders we see in our Secret Place. It may well be that true naturalists would be aghast at our interpretations of the things we see. If we encounter a bird unnoticed on other days, we enjoy it. It has given us a moment of beauty, though we don't even know its name. It has gifted us with a memory and memories need no names.

A rainbow needs no reason for its existence. It is there. Enjoy it, savor it. There may be a logical explanation why the crow's harsh croak is less musical than the lilt of a wren. But, to the crows, its voice is not a croak nor is it harsh. It is a crow's song and it is sung proudly.

One of the fascinating happenings we might like to explore further is the long sleep of hibernation. We don't know which creatures practice suspended animation nor how long those that do hibernate are in the state that is neither life nor death.

We have sat by the campfire talking of how the world might be changed in our sight if we, too, practiced hibernation. Things we know and love would be altered when we awoke for time would not have stood still as we slept. We wonder if our hills and woods might be given over to houses and garages and asphalt driveways.

Discussing hibernation leads our thoughts to speculating on what happens to the creatures we observe on our hikes.

It is said some insects live only a few hours while some lives span a matter of days. None live past the last warm days of autumn. When the winds of early winter sweep across our hill, they bring the touch of death to hordes of grasshoppers, woolly worms, crickets and all the other insects that swarm away from our passing as we tramp through the tall summer grasses. Grasshoppers are the most noticeable, because they are so large, but there are others, millions of others, in the meadows and in the bushes at the side of the Okaw.

The warmth leaves, and so does life for the insect

world, but we wonder where all the millions of bodies are left. Except for an occasional grasshopper or cricket, we have yet to see winter-killed remains of any of the untold numbers of victims.

One unusually cold day in early fall, we hiked past the sassafrass grove and through the stand of tall trees where the rabbit had fooled the big dog. There is a deep ravine at the north end of the meadow adjoining the grove. This ravine is sheltered on each side by thick oak trees and the winds seldom disturb the floor of the gully.

One day we saw a 'possum walking along the edge of the ditch that has helped carve the ravine. The little gray animal was unhurried and stopped to sniff at each bush and tree. It was so intent on its afternoon stroll and on inspecting the undergrowth that it never noticed the two observers. It disappeared under the bushes that line the ravine near the river's edge.

We decided to build a fire in that sheltered place and warm our hands and feet. There might be a happening if we observed for long enough.

After our blaze was going, we sat with our backs against the trees and our boot-soles scant inches from the fire talking of many things.

I scratched at the dead leaves with my staff. Presently, I showed Steven half a dozen little lady bugs I had uncovered. They were frantically scurrying back under other piles of leaves. We continued turning leaves over and discovered there were hundreds of the little things snuggled under them in a ten foot area around our fire. There was an occasional "stink bug," looming tall among its smaller companions.

We wondered if this were hibernation or a last desperate stand against the inevitable winds and cold. Perhaps there are hardy bugs of other species that spend the bitter midwest winter in long, warm sleep.

These are questions left unanswered. We watched awhile, then extinguished our fire, covered the bugs, and walked to the river, talking of what we had seen.

Motivation

IT IS NO SECRET that we humans act irrationally at times. Motivated by anger or frustration, we break the pattern of predictable behavior and do things out of character with our normal personality.

Although Steven and I project human reactions and feelings onto the animals we observe, we know a wild creature is not an individual but a member of a species. Each species has evolved into a set pattern of conduct. A squirrel is a member of the squirrel family and does squirrel things. Reality tells us that squirrels gather nuts and store them into remembered caches, gather, not from a sense of thrift, but because gathering nuts is an instinctive activity of squirrels. A fox behaves in the manner of all foxes. All animals within a species behave like all other members of that species. Their instinctive reactions are born of centuries of evolution.

However, we have seen creatures of the Secret Place do strange things that do not seem to follow a set pattern, and we wonder at the motivation that triggers such things.

Late one afternoon we were at the corner of the lane where it meets the road that passes our house. There had been a brief rain shower and the oiled road glistened in the half light of early evening. We knew the banks of the river would be dry as it takes a heavy rain to filter through the trees along the water's edge, for the leaves are thick and sheltering. We also knew the bushes and weeds on the way to the Place would be rain-soaked and that our trousers and socks would be uncomfortable in a matter of a few seconds' walking. But the fish are most active after a summer shower and the night seemed to promise a time of interesting observation, so we decided on a night hike into the Secret Place.

As we paused at the corner before beginning our walk, we noticed a movement in the wet grass at the side of the road. We have learned that if we detect motion in the grass or under the trees, the wisest action is to stand absolutely motionless on the chance that whatever caused the movement will go about its business and can be watched.

In a few seconds, we saw a small frog, no larger than a man's thumb, hop from the roadside and travel west to east, toward the river. Its body shone with moisture from the weeds.

Much of a frog's travelling time is consumed by a waiting period it observes between hops. It will hop- . . . pause . . . hop . . . pause. We think the wait between hops may be to allow the frog to consider its next move or to check the weeds ahead for danger. This one never paused in its journey across the roadway. It never rested between hops but stretched its little body in the longest possible leaps. It was intent on its destination.

Then a second frog came hopping from the weeds in the same general area as the first. The first one had not disappeared into the weeks on the east side of the road before the second made its appearance. It was going in the same direction and seemed to possess the same sense of urgency as the first. As we stood and watched, we saw there were many frogs crossing the road. Each was small and each was hopping toward the river and none paused between hops but hurried across the slick, oiled road. It was an awesome experience to watch those determined little creatures.

We wondered where all those little frogs had lived before they began their mass migration. We wondered what they would do after they arrived and if they realized the great distance they must travel.

Inevitably, a car passed going north at great speed. We watched helplessly as scores of the tiny creatures were crushed beneath the tires. Still they came, leaping over the broken bodies in the road and disappearing into the wet weeds on the other side.

We wondered what call was sounded to move those little frogs to defy distance and death.

There is a half acre plot of lawn adjoining our house on the north. It is a place with many anthills half hidden in the grass, and a home for big, fat bumblebees and an occasional snake. The half acre was a splendid place for exploration when the boy's legs were short and the river seemed far away.

More than one covey of quail has used that open stretch of ground for a runway. They come from the fence-row back of our house and move to shelter in the thick woods across the road. They run swiftly and furtively, in short dashes, single file, heads bobbing, until they reach the roadside, then cross one at a time. Quail are more traffic-wise than the larger, slower pheasants. We have seen many pheasants which had been killed by cars, but few quail. They do not sound their distinctive "Bob White" call until the entire family is safe in the thick bushes and high weeds.

Sometimes a rabbit will use the corner of our lot as a short cut to the meadow. It will pause to nibble awhile at the clover, then go about its rabbit routine. Rabbits are slow moving creatures: they never display their capacity for speed until a chase begins.

When the lawn is being mowed in the later afternoon, martins swoop down and catch bugs alarmed into flight by the whirling blades. Martins are used to people: they come very close to us as we ride the mower.

We saw a happening on this small plot of ground that rivalled the frog migration.

We came home from the nearby town late one evening. The glare from our headlights flashed across the lawn as we turned our car into the driveway. A full moon lit the road and meadow and distorted tree-shadows darkened the lane.

It was such a clear night we could see the top of our Amish neighbor's silo, a half mile to the north.

We noticed a movement on the lawn and walked across the driveway in order to observe more closely.

We stared in disbelief. A rabbit was doing things no rabbit would be expected to do. It leapt into the air and as it fell back to the ground, it would lash out its hind legs with a vicious kick. The rabbit danced a crazy dance, up and down and around, kicking and leaping as it went.

After a moment we noticed our dancer was not alone in its moonlight madness. There were at least a dozen other rabbits on that lawn, each leaping and circling and kicking. Around and around they went;

we stood entranced. A car approached and our strange dancers vanished.

We like to think that rabbits meet at other times and in other places to dance the night away, with no human noises or cars to disturb their revelry.

Is it a ritual dance, or do they leap for the sheer joy of leaping? Are some rabbits more accomplished than others and do they find themselves in great demand at all the rabbit parties?

Habits

OUR TRIPS TO the Secret Place normally follow a set pattern. We begin at the pool that was home for the family of silent bullfrogs. We walk down the lane past the thicket that shelters quail in the winter time. We pass the squared gate post by the Amishman's horse pasture. We climb two barbed wire fences and walk through the grove of sapling trees to the well-worn path at the river's edge, which we follow to the campsite.

We seldom break that routine. If Steven hikes alone, I almost always know where he will be. Occasionally one of us will leave half an hour ahead of the other and mark a trail to be followed. The tracker must be alert for broken tree limbs and small bark-slashes if he is to follow the trail to the other's hiding place. We find we are apt to follow our accustomed path even while playing the tracking game. We are all creatures of habit.

We are able to watch the wild creatures, because they are creatures of habit, too.

There are certain areas in the Place where we are most likely to see rabbits than in other areas; they live in those areas and rabbits are home-loving animals. For example, if we scare up a rabbit as we walk across the meadow east of the bottom-land maple grove, we know to wait awhile and it will return to the place where we startled it into flight. It will usually run north toward the cabin, cross the meadow, run along the crest of our hill, then back to the maple grove. This is a dangerous route for the rabbit to follow in hunting season. The hunter's dog will follow at the heels of the terrified rabbit and keep it moving until the circle has been completed and the chase ends where the hunter is waiting with his gun.

Thor, the hawk, circles our meadow awhile, then moves across the river to hunt over another field. The big bird does not always hunt over one small area, but follows a criss-cross pattern in its flight. When one hunting ground has been systematically searched, it is time to move on. We think that if we clocked the time Thor spent over each field, we would discover a definite time pattern to the hawk's day.

Domesticated animals also live by routine. The daily visits of our neighbor's dog have worn a path in our lawn. When we hike along the river bank in areas outside our Secret Place, we cross pasture lands and see where cows have worn deep paths in the grass and the top soil. Each morning's journey from the barn to the grazing place and each journey back in the evening follows the same trail. Farm wives who raise orphaned pigs find it best to feed the motherless animals according to a set schedule.

A good fisherman learns to read the river. Fish are more likely to feed when the river is rising from a recent rain than when it is falling during a dry period. It is a good idea to cast at the mouth of any stream that feeds the Okaw as the fish come to an outlet to feed on worms and bugs washed down from the fields. Catfish and carp frequent the deeper holes near untidy log jams while drum fish prefer swifter flowing waters. Crappie like to congregate around submerged trees in lakes.

Birds are not the free-flying souls one often imagines, but recognize and defend well-defined boundaries. Much of the singing we hear in the Secret Place are warning cries and territorial declarations. The big owl has lived in the same grove of trees for several years. We have seen it only once or twice but we hear its deep voice in the night and its presence is betrayed by the droppings beneath its nesting tree.

Wrens return to the same house year after year. When sparrows become accustomed to roosting in a particular tree or barn, the homing habit is so strong, it becomes a continuing battle to get rid of them. Sparrows are bold and aggressive birds and would probably be appreciated more if they did not flock in such great numbers.

Robins appear on schedule each morning and each afternoon to wrestle night crawlers from our yard beneath the apple tree. An interesting robin family lived near us at one time. There were three in the family: two mates and an apparent friend. We supposed the friend had lost its mate and had moved in with the others out of loneliness. For a while there was harmony in the little group as they searched for bugs and worms; then one morning one of the mated pair soundly thrashed the odd one and sent it to the corner of the yard in disgrace. After a little while, the three were working together again.

A tribe of blue jays arrives at our house at the same time each morning to feast on the food we have scattered outside. They leave and the scavenger birds take over.

Although we know what we are looking for and where we will find it, the thrill is never routine. It is always new and filled with wonder.

Living off the land

"LIVING OFF THE LAND" is a phrase that fascinates us. We visualize free souls who forsake much of modern society and learn to make do without the trappings of less hardy folk. In a way, we envy those who have acquired the skill of making soap, rooting medicinal herbs, cooking on wood-burning stoves and practicing other crafts now kept alive by interest rather than by necessity. Our Amish neighbors live close to the ways of yesterday. They farm with horses, live in houses with no utilities and shun many of the luxuries we have come to consider necessities. But even the Amish use shopping centers and supermarkets.

The Secret Place offers much to one who yearns after a way of life more primitive than that of the Amish.

The list of available foodstuffs in the Secret Place is endless. Some we know very well. There are others that we can't find or don't know how to use.

The sassafrass grove yields a fine beverage. We clean and boil the red-hued roots of that lovely small tree; our kitchen is filled with its sweet licorice aroma. The early settlers were convinced that drinking great quantities of sassafrass tea thinned one's blood and warded off colds and the "shakes." The tea is probably as efficient as many high-priced pills and liquids sold for the same purpose. The roots are free for the digging. We brew and drink sassafrass tea for its sweet taste, rather than for any medicinal purpose.

Blackberries and dew berries as large as a man's thumb grow in thick patches along the lane and in the woods at the edge of the river. Thorns, tickle grass and chiggers are constant companions to the juicy berries but the flavor is worth the discomfort.

Wild strawberries crowd the weeds along the banks of the ditch leading to the thicket. Although much smaller than the domesticated variety, they taste better than the ones from the supermarket. And they are free.

Wild onions flourish in the ravine north of the sassafrass grove. They are smaller than the onions tended in our gardens but years of growing without cultivation has not diminished their taste.

There are many varities of hickory tree, from the huge "scaly barks" to the "pigs." There are not as many walnut trees, but they are prolific and the harvest is plentiful.

Persimmon and paw paw trees grow along the river north of the Secret Place.

A growth of crabapple trees stands in the horse pasture and their blossoms speckle the grass with touches of color when they fall.

Channel catfish grow to ten or twelve pounds in the river and carp are even heavier. Thick-bodied drumfish strike viciously at nightcrawlers and bullfrogs sing around the pond night and day.

Gray and fox squirrel work the nut trees in the forest, and pheasant and quail nest in the meadows.

The rabbits have always been with us and now we have deer.

This free menu offers more than sustenance. There is an endless variety of choices and taste.

However, the Secret Place sets its table according to a plan and that plan is not easy to live with. There is a a time and a place for each thing.

Sassafrass roots are dug only a few weeks of the year. Strawberries and blackberries, along with persimmon and paw paw, have a special time for living and giving—and then dying.

Fish bite mainly when they are hungry. The river freezes and the crawdaddies and the frogs and most of those that live in the water go into their long sleep. Carp bury themselves in the mud bottom to wait out the season.

The only food that may be gathered at all times is the hickory nut and even this diet may be precarious. Snow covers the ground beneath the nut trees and the ground itself freezes solid, imprisoning the unshelled nuts.

Sitting by the campfire in our heavy clothing over insulated underwear, with our gloved hands held out to the fire, we are grateful for things as they are.

We will leave living off the land to those made of sterner stuff.

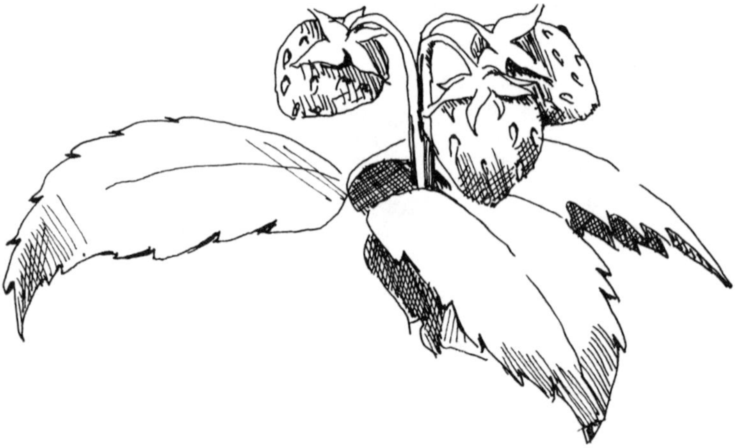

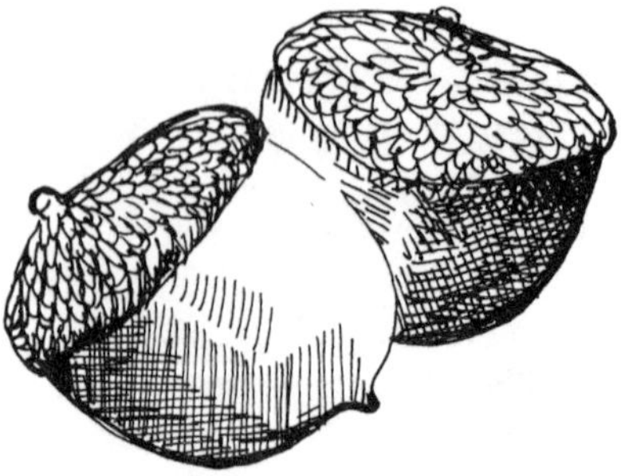

To Run or To Hide

WILD THINGS IN the Place must make a life or death decision when the unexpected happens. When stalked by an enemy or chanced upon by observers like ourselves, the creature must burst into instant flight or practice the art of absolute immobility. If the reaction to danger is controlled by instinct, then instinct allows a choice.

Sudden movement can be fatal. Many times we have passed a wooded area unaware that we were being watched by fearful eyes, until the watcher moved in its shelter. It takes much courage to remain quiet and motionless as the sound of death moves closer to the clump of weeds in which a creature is hiding. A rabbit's heart must pound as it flattens itself beneath a bush, its leg muscles taut in readiness for that first frantic leap. It must make an instinctive decision whether to spring now and risk a chase or to still its thumping heart and outwait the enemy.

We believe instinct allows a third choice in some cases. The hunted may startle and confuse the hunter. Perhaps the pheasant rockets skyward with a nerve-shattering whirr of its wings to gain a precious second of time. Ask any hunter the number of times he has been shocked into an early, futile shot. This is why hunters work with dogs, for dogs use ancient cunning, as well as their senses, to point out the hiding place so that the hunter will be ready when the pheasant takes wing.

Suppose, just suppose, we tell each other, instinct allowed yet another choice: the choice of fighting back.

If all the rabbits we see as we cross the meadow west of the cottonwood were to make the decision that enough is enough, it is time to make a stand, how quickly hunting routines would be altered! We think no dog could survive an attack by a dozen buck rabbits, each lashing out with those powerful hind legs. There is not only safety in numbers but there is also strength, and there are far more rabbits than dogs in the meadows in hunting season.

We can imagine a hunter and his dog stalking a covey of quail. Just suppose the covey could also stalk and attack. Think of the wild retreat of the hunter and his crestfallen dog before the onslaught of a covey of outraged quail.

But the rules of instinct are inflexible and its choices are few.

Many a laurel wreath has been placed on the brow of a man who has reacted from sheer fright and allowed bravery to take credit for the deed. Man may be the only animal that concerns himself with what others may think of his bravery. No other animal is afraid to run or hide when faced with a foe. The creatures who share our world know nothing of laurel wreaths or of bravery so they continue to make the choice of running or hiding.

Wild things are not as clever at concealment as one might think. Some are blessed with coloration that blends with the environment while others possess the facility of changing colors to fit the background. Others are conspicuous against any background. We can follow the flight of a cardinal through the thickest woods but a thrush may perch in the browned leaves of a dying tree and we never suspect how near we are to its hiding place. A quail running ahead of us in the meadow is invisible in a matter of seconds.

We have watched spiders scuttle ahead of us in woodland paths. A spider normally takes refuge under a fallen leaf. Although most of its body is exposed, it thinks itself well hidden and will remain under its imagined covering until danger is past. We place our staffs on the ground near the leaf and tap close to the spider's body, but it never moves.

A rabbit cowers in a clump of weeds as we draw near. It considers itself well camouflaged, but we can see it quite plainly. It makes the life or death decision to wait us out and flattens itself against the ground, nose twitching, until we can almost touch it. Only then does it explode into the open field in panic-stricken flight.

A squirrel would seem most blessed of all creatures with opportunity for cover and concealment. It escapes to a tall forest oak and hides in a jagged clump of leaves very nearly the color of its own fur.

Many times it foolishly allows its long, bushy tail to droop from the limb like a flag signalling its presence. The squirrel is an inquisitive animal and we will often attract it to our own hiding place by rhythmically tapping the side of a tree with our staff. It will forget its fear and come from its hiding place to investigate the sound.

Not every animal excels at its tribal craft any more than each human excels at his. Wild things can make errors that may cost them their lives.

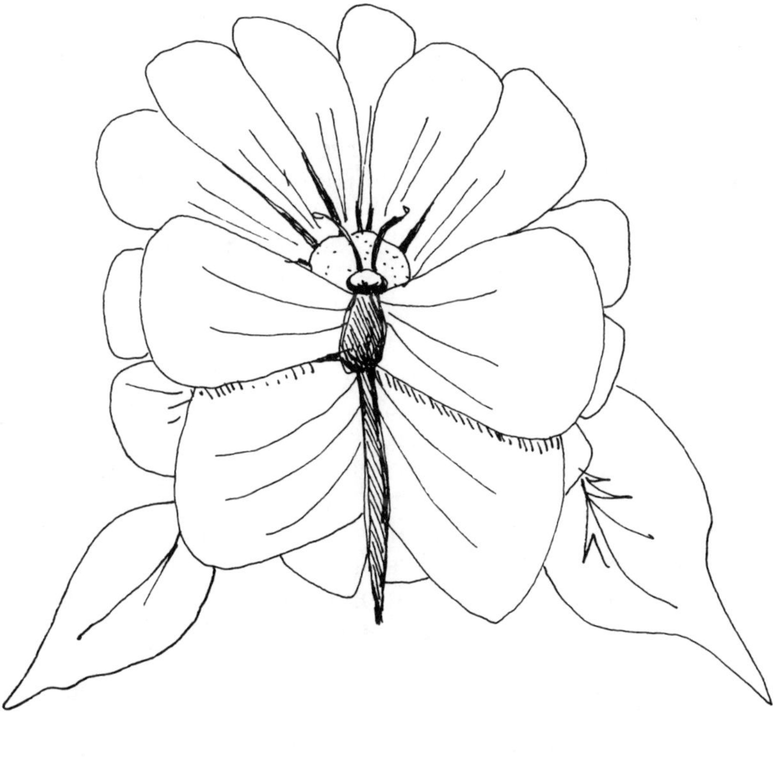

Hiking Gear

SINCE THE SECRET PLACE is close to our home and relatively small in area, we have no need for long-distance backpacking gear. A leisurely fifteen minute hike brings us to the heart of the Secret Place. It is not distance that makes a hike successful, but the number of happenings one observes.

We have sat on a log at any one of our observation points and watched countless lives being lived. The earth, a dead log, the sky, the surface of the water—each shares the complexities of its world with one who will take the time to watch and to study and to care. A hurried, unseeing walk is worse than no walk at all, for the creatures are frightened of sound and movement. Many worlds evolve in a city park, unnoticed by those who hurry past to watch the caged animals in the zoo. Once we sat warming in the sunshine on the river bank. A turtle floated downstream, hardly moving its feet. A crawdaddy backed along the river bottom, inches under the surface. A bird clung to a limb scarcely three feet from our heads and ran through its repertoire of songs. A muskrat busied itself, twenty feet upstream. I turned to Steven and remarked, "This is the way it was meant to be." As I moved and spoke, the magic disappeared. There was the river and the trees and the sunlight, but the worlds were gone.

We always carry binoculars for, as much as we wish otherwise, we are not an accepted part of the worlds we watch. A whispered word, a slight movement, and that world escapes. With binoculars we place ourselves in a distant world which goes about its business unaware that we are watching.

We take matches for fire building. Our fires are not for warmth alone; few things are as stimulating to long thoughts and conversations as a fire at the river's edge. At night, we feel other eyes studying our fires and we hear twigs snapping and bushes rustling in the darkness.

We are never without our staffs. Steven and I differ in our choice of walking sticks. I carry an ordinary cane with a crooked handle that is useful for snagging floating objects from the river. It may also be used as a golf club on cans and small rocks and the tip is the right size for probing snake and crawfish holes. I tell Steven my cane may appear flimsy, but it is sturdy and conveys a certain air of elegance. Steven is loyal to his own staff, a larger, more rugged one, cut from a tree limb. He says its size and shape would make it the choice of a real woodsman.

Although there is little likelihood we will be forced to defend ourselves with our staffs, there is a kind of comfort in the feel of the wood as we hike through the more rugged areas of the Secret Place. It is not beyond the realm of possibility that a mother fox or some other creature will decide we are some place we should not be, as indeed we are. There has been talk of dog packs running at night and we have seen signs of their communal cruelty. We found the skeleton of a small dog we had known very well. Its neck had been snapped; it could be identified only by patches of fur.

A staff is not the ultimate weapon. The one we could carry to prove our superiority over the wild things hangs on a wall at home. It has not been fired in many years.

Our gear is inexpensive and unsophisticated, but it is all we need in the Secret Place.

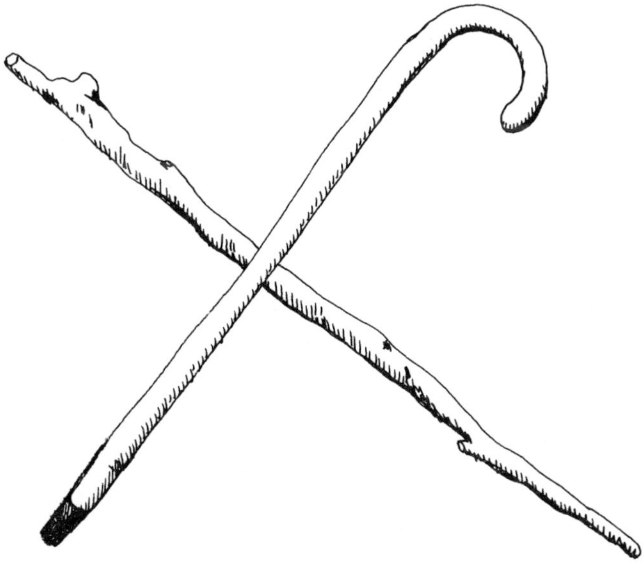

The Web Weavers

CREATURES IN THE Secret Place wear the personalities we choose to give them, and the giving enhances our watching. We can imagine cunning and laughter and love in the actions of the wild things and the imagining helps us feel we are a part of their living. We can manufacture a closeness to the creatures that is dear to us, even though it is not mutual.

The world of Thor, the hawk, is not really our world, for the big bird does not recognize our existence. He seems to notice us only when we hike across the meadow and disturb his hunting. But we bestow on Thor a feeling of friendship for us and also a sense of loneliness. He becomes our friend in our minds, and we think that he misses us on the days when we do not come to the Secret Place.

Mrs. Green, the snake, is totally unaware of our kinship with her. We would feel a genuine sense of loss if she were not in her usual patch of weeds, but if we were never again to walk down the lane past her home, she would not wonder at our absence. She is a friend in our own minds and that is sufficient for us.

The family of bull frogs that once lived across the road feared us as they feared all humans and unexpected noises and movement. They were a source of wonder to us and because of that wonder we moved a little closer to their world.

If we fabricate a friendship, bestow a gift of speech or thought, or even of love, our Secret Place and its creatures become more meaningful.

One of the creatures of the Secret Place lives in a world in which we have never attempted to feel a sense of belonging. We feel no closeness to the spider family.

Spiders belong to a tribe of marvellously constructed beings, more enduring than most living things on earth. The artistry of the spider's craft is unquestioned and its society complex beyond imagining. I have never touched a spider.

We carefully check leaves and grasses where spiders may be working. Our dislike comes close to fear.

Despite our aversion to spiders, they afford us hours of pleasure. We watch as they spin their lovely webs, so fragile yet so strong. We find their handiwork in all areas of the Secret Place. Sometimes they build high off the ground in corners of the cabin's porch roof. Some webs are tethered to low bushes and weeds, inches off the forest floor. Others seem to float on the tops of weeds and they glisten with dew many hours after sunrise. We feel the soft touch of webs as we hike through the woods; these have ben strung from branch to branch. The spiders must have used great strength and swung unbelievable distances to accomplish that engineering marvel. Some webs lie horizontal and others stand perpendicular. Some are cone-shaped and we can see the spider lying in wait at the small end, like the malevolent creature most people think him to be.

One normally does not think of spiders as separate individuals, but those we watch seem to follow no set pattern of behavior. Webs are spun in varying styles of architecture and in differing locations. Even the strategy of their attack differs. Some wait in the corner of the web as the victim thrashes about. Others move slowly across the strands and take a position at the side of their prey and watch its struggles. Still others spring viciously at the first sign of entanglement and inject venom again and again.

We had thought that entrapment in the web spelled certain death for any insect, but many escaped, some quite easily. The larger ones, such as grasshoppers, bullied their way through the sticky threads and dropped to the ground beneath. Many of the smaller insects simply walked across the web, like the spider itself, and rolled over the edge. We have seen insects break through the web to safety and then leap back into it again, perhaps confused by panic. The spider's success in hunting seems no greater than that of any other creature: just as hawks sometimes miss their targets and rabbits elude dogs, spiders lose their victims.

Oddly enough, at times the spider makes no attempt to attack its struggling victim but watches from its corner as though the hunter were frightened of the hunted. Perhaps some of the insects caught in the trap are unpalatable, perhaps some are capable of defense, even when shackled by the fine threads. For whatever reason, the spider waits and watches, motionless, as its web is ripped and shattered by the prey. It makes no attempt to attack.

There is much repair work to be done after each encounter, regardless of whether a kill is made. There must be a mending of holes and gashes, a tying of loose ends. The spiders do this slowly and with great skill. We have seen them drag heavy bodies across the small threads of the trap and never disturb a single strand.

We watch the spiders with respect and appreciation, but we always find outselves rooting for the other side.

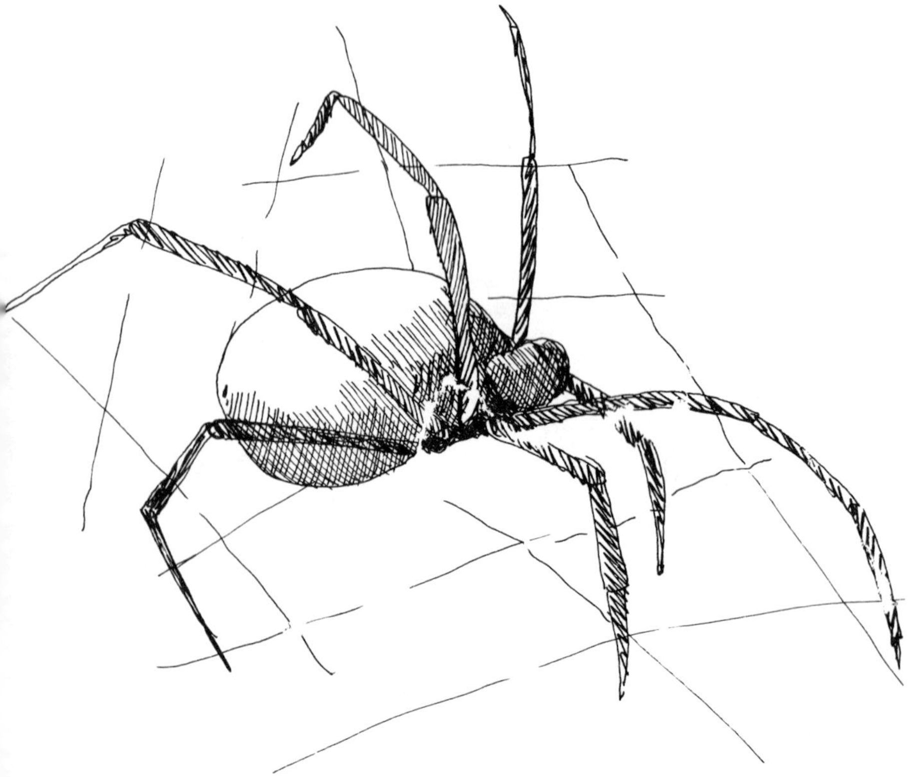

Acrobats and Swimmers

ANT-WATCHING WAS the first of our adventures. In our yard, as in most, there are many hills and cities. We discovered that a few grains of sugar spread around a colony started a chain reaction of carrying and storing and bustling around. There was much bickering over the sugar grains and some thievery. Ants are possibly the busiest creatures in the Secret Place; they are acknowledged workaholics, but their work seems to lack definite direction.

We have watched a big black ant tiptoe the length of a branch projecting over the river. It hung over the edge of the last leaf, and began a series of inane gymnastics. All alone, far out over the water, it entertained itself by wildly waving its extremities and running back and forth. We wondered what possible motivation of instinct or evolution could inspire such antics.

After the show was over, the ant returned to the bank and wandered around, with much backtracking and retracing of steps. Much has been written about the ants' highly developed society; those we observed seem to live in a confused state.

Once we saw an ant marooned on a floating maple leaf. The fragile craft was threatened with disaster at any moment by the swirling waves, but the ant never ceased to move slowly back and forth across the leaf.

Steven made an attempt to bring the leaf to shore with his staff: the ant was washed overboard into the quiet shallows along the river's edge. It struck out strongly toward a small branch lying half in the water, half on the shore. After reaching safety, it walked to the bank and began the familiar backtracking and circling.

We wondered what would have happened to the ant if it had not been swept from its leaf. Perhaps it would have been carried downstream to a far off log jam or sand bar. Would it have waded ashore and joined a new colony? Would the stranger from the waters have been accepted by other ants or other cities? It surely would not have spent the rest of its days without other ants and ant hills.

Ant societies have been said to be close-knit, but we have seen little evidence of their concern for one another.

When one area of the colony is disturbed, the other areas will go about their business as though nothing was happening to their companions. A bit of food is fought over by family members as though it were not a communal goal to carry it to the storage room.

Ants cannot abide inactivity. Pick one from a dead tree, place it on the ground a few feet from its home and it instantly starts its characteristic wandering. It seems to forget where it was going, but hurries anyway. Carry it even further away and it hustles around as though the new area was where it wanted to go all along. No moments of meditation or quiet reflection for our friend, the ant.

There is a four foot square metal plate lying on the ground in front of the cabin porch. We were watching the river from the bluffs one Saturday and walked back to turn the plate over for we had seen a snake hiding under it on a previous hike and thought it might be sheltering there again.

Underneath, there was a colony of large red ants at one end and one of smaller black ants at the other. When the sun hit their exposed shelter, there was great agitation in each colony. Despite much rushing around and wringing of hands, not once did either of the two groups invade the other's territory. We picked up a large red one and dropped it into the enemy's camp. It scrambled frantically, trying to find its way to its own corner, losing its way several times in the process. The smaller ants seemed more preoccupied with their disorganized scurrying than with repelling the invader. Some of them ran to look at and to touch the big red stranger, but showed no animosity.

One Saturday morning, we built a fire, using dead logs we had found near the campsite. As we sat watching the blaze, we noticed some ants on one of the logs. We quickly brushed them off on to the ground but we were unable to reach one of them because of the flames. As we watched, the ant ran to the end of its log, stared at the flames a moment and then began the gymnastics we had seen performed on the branch over the river. It could easily have walked down a limb leading to the ground without being singed, but it did its dance as the flames licked closer. We brushed it off the log and as soon as it landed, it began its purposeless wandering.

Ants possess an enviable reputation for thrift and hard work, but they seem to lack a definite goal.

The Pack

IT TAKES US longer to return from the river than to get there. Our steps are slower and we linger over the scenery. We rest often, although we are not tired. After we reach the top of the hill and say goodbye to the cottonwood and start down the lane, we know another adventure is about to become a memory.

There was one dark night, however, when we made the trip home in less time than we would have ever believed possible.

It was a night hike and we have said before that shadows and sounds take on new meanings in the dark. Even our familiar hill joins in the conspiracy to confuse us with unfamiliar shapes. The world of the Secret Place with its shadows and night noises lies before us as we stand at the crest of the hill. We hear the sounds of grazing in the pasture although it is too dark for us to see the horses themselves.

A few hundred feet to the north, the sassafrass grove has blended into the shadows of the hickorys and oaks. Only patches of the cottonwood's white bark is visible. Behind us, there are lights and people, cars on country roads and we hear the rhythmic clop, clop of horses' hooves on oiled surface. It is as though we are standing between reality and make-believe, which, indeed, we are.

On such a night, we had spent an hour or two at the campfire, listening to the river and the soft sounds of the night things. The big owl had called many times and the lesser members of its tribe had answered each call. We did some answering also, but as Steven remarked, it would have required a very young owl to have been deceived by our bird calls.

It had been a successful night hike: we had heard the call of whippoorwills in the woods across from our house. In spite of the melancholy tone of their cries, the whippoorwills are sweet-singing birds.

We decided to return home by way of the cabin trail, since the meadow would be more easily travelled than the woods in the unusually dark night. The river paths are difficult to follow without flashing our lights, but much of the thrill of night hiking comes from moving in the dark, as the wild things do.

We were reluctant to leave, so we walked slowly past the big logjam with the deep fishing hole where the battered jon boat rocks with the current. We could hear the splash of big carp as they leaped in the river and a dozen bull frogs squealed and splashed from the banks ahead of us. Do they always squeal from fright or is it also a warning call to other frogs?

There was a mild south wind and occasionally one tree limb swayed against another, creating an eerie, whining sound. Although we know the sound well, it is always startling and our conversations become more hushed as though we are in the presence of a mystery.

That night, we were half way up the meadow slope, nearing the cabin, when we first heard the pack. It was a chorus sung by many dogs, coming toward the Secret Place.

If one listens closely, it is obvious that dogs' voices carry a wide range of emotions. They bark differently when they chase cars than when they tree cats. A happy welcome home is far removed from the surly warning against trespass.

It is a pleasure to sit by the campfire at night and listen to the sounds of the dogs in Cooks Mills. First, we may hear a long deep bark, almost a howl. We know this is a hound, tied in a back yard, but remembering chases under a harvest moon. The answer is a high pitched staccatto yelping, repeated many times. This is a house dog, out for a stroll in the evening, reminding its friends that although it has never known the thrill of the hunt, it can still speak the language.

The dog sounds we hear at the campfire speak of people and lighted windows and much loved family pets. Sounds carry far on the river at night and they are normally pleasant and familiar sounds.

The sounds we heard that night were not pleasant ones.

The music of a dog pack comes in three separate phases. First, the sound of the hunt. Nothing has been sighted or smelled and one can visualize the dogs walking or trotting slowly, noses to the ground, speaking to one another. Some of the dogs move silently and range ahead and to the side of the others. There is a sense of intense concentration and there will be head-to-head conferences over cold trails.

Next, comes the chase, for a trail has been found. First one dog, then another, sounds the cry; the pack joins in. The dogs begin to run now, and the tone changes to an excited chorus. One can almost see them jumping logs and bushes, bullying their way through tall weeds and thick underbrush. Some are longer-winded and better runners than others and the pack is widely separated.

Then, the kill. If the quarry is a tree climber, the barks sound frustrated and angry. If the prey is surrounded and brought to the ground, the air is filled with snarls and fierce yelps.

The dogs we heard that night were still hunting and coming toward the river. We had never heard of dogs attacking humans in our countryside, but our steps quickened.

The noisy mob was on the other side of the river and not coming directly toward us, but rivers can be swum and directions can be changed. We walked even faster. Cool reason changes to chilling speculation when a boy and his grandfather are blessed with a vivid imagination.

We wondered if our friend, the big black dog, were a member of the pack. We didn't know if he would remember our hours of companionship or be moved by the blood lust that grips undisciplined mobs. Perhaps he would stand between us and his howling friends; perhaps he would lead the charge.

We decided on a full flight across the meadow.

We had not known the meadow was so full of grasping thorn bushes and uneven hillocks and tough weed patches. The patch through the sassafrass grove seemed endless.

Through the trees and into the fresh-picked corn field we fled, with the corn stubble snapping beneath our feet and the dust churning around our pants legs.

It was then we heard the tones change to the sounds of the chase. The dogs seemed to be running past the place where the jon boat rides in the river.

On we ran, toward the lights of home, with the dogs baying along the river and unnamed terrors at our heels.

I became aware that although Steven is young and fleet of foot, and I am neither, I was far ahead of him. Panic-stricken at the thought that we might be separated, I stopped running. He stopped, also. I realized then that he was placing himself between the dogs and me. I had never experienced a more moving moment in all our years in the Secret Place; I ran the rest of the way home with a lump crowding my throat. We finished our wild flight side by side.

Of course, we reached home safely, panting, and full of our adventure.

When we tell our tale of the wild pack, some might wonder how many dogs we actually saw. Perhaps, they say, we heard a few hounds chasing a tired old raccoon, rather than the wild bunch gathering for a chase. Were we alone in that mad run across the corn stubble, or did we add the dogs and the dark night and the river sounds and arrive at an unreal answer? We don't want to know how many dogs there were or what they were doing or if they even knew we were there.

It is a grand memory and it matters little to us how much of that memory is imagination.

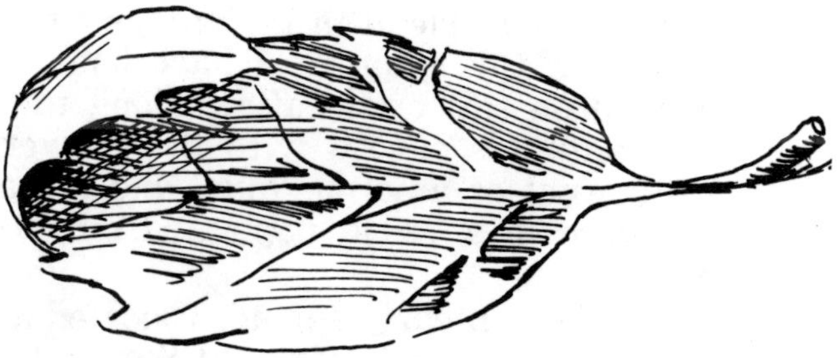

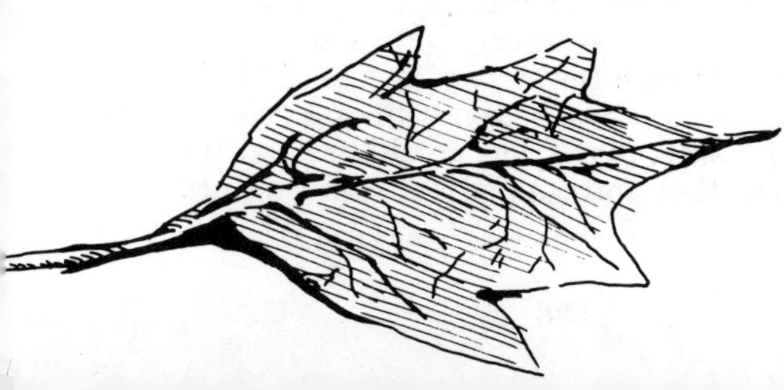

The Flute Maker

I SUPPOSE NO ONE knows who, in what time, first fashioned a musical instrument. Whether carved of bone or whittled from wood, the finished product must have been handled with loving care by that father or mother of all musicians. The hands that shaped the first flute were those of an artist; one who thinks with his hands brings dreams to life just as those whose art is expressed in words or notes or brush strokes.

We think it would have been great fun to watch the reactions of the family of the first flutist as he coaxed melodies from the strange new toy. Diligent practice works wonders in improving musical talent, but it has been known to strain family relationships.

It is almost certain that the first woodland flute was built in the same manner and in the same shape as the last. The construction of a crude flute appears childishly simple. I have watched it done many times and all that is required is a sharp pocket knife and a branch approximately one half inch in diameter.

The branch is cut from a sapling tree when the underlying bark is wet with rising sap. A few deft slashes with the knife, some taps on the bark to loosen it and make it slide easily off the branch, a straight edge sliced along the top of the barkless branch, a few holes drilled into the sleeve of the bark. . .slide the bark back on to the branch, and we have the basic woodland flute.

We have a friend in the village who builds quail callers in this manner. I have listened as he performed on this crude affair along the river bank. The flatlands echoed with the answering calls of belligerent or amorous quail and it was as though we were in a world populated only by very loud quail.

One day, in early spring, I located a sapling just the right size, and informed Steven I was about to make a flute. He seemed properly impressed.

I mentally ran through the steps of successful flute construction and set to work with my knife. Pretending as long as possible that I was an old hand at the flute craft, I whittled and tapped and shaved until something vaguely resembling a flute rested in my hands.

It was neither a flute nor a quail call; it was a piece of wood and entertained no further ambition. I could call forth no sound of any kind.

I wasted most of that morning carving at sap-oozing tree limbs while the river flowed and the fish leaped and the birds sang and there was so much I could have seen and shared.

There were certain remarks from Steven and my frustration grew with each futile effort.

If the creatures possess a sense of humor, how they must have enjoyed the spectacle of a gray-headed man sitting on a log by the river side, whittling and blowing on pieces of trees.

No mention was made of my fiasco on the way home, but I could see an occasional smile cross Steven's face as though he were thinking of something funny.

Perhaps, one of these days I will ask my friend at Cooks Mills to teach me the art of making quail callers. The next weekend I will casually create a flute from a tree branch and give a little concert by the side of the Okaw.

Maybe I will tell Steven how I improved in my craft and maybe I will not.

On this day, however, I satisfied my musical craving by placing a broadleafed weed between my thumbs and blowing lustily across the top. This takes no artistic nor musical talent and produces a sound not unlike the call of a crow.

I suspect many of our ancestors may have left off making flutes to do the same.

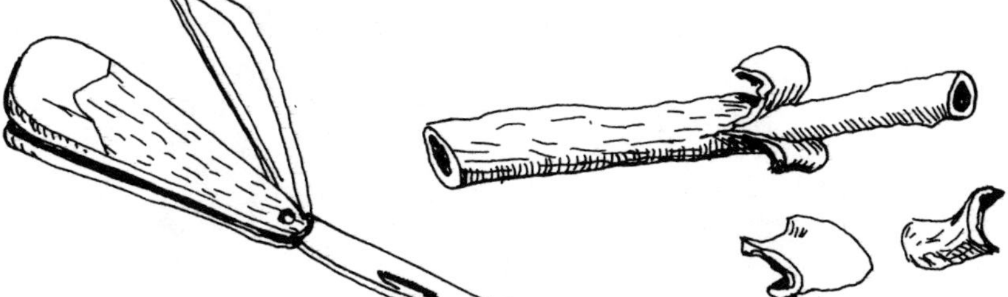

Changes

STEVEN HAS BEEN following the progress of our journal with much interest. He asks how an end can come to the Secret Place, even in a book. Secret Places live as long as the mind lives that creates them. The world of our Secret Place is the river and the woods and the meadow. There are other Secret Places in other worlds, created by other minds.

Our Secret Place was where it is long before we learned to love it and it will be as it is long after we leave it. Love of Secret Places is not confined to one family or to one place. Appreciation of wonders is not an unshared emotion. In our minds, we have counted the creatures and wild things as our special friends. If someone else becomes a part of that world as we did, they will be watched, as we were, in fear. Whoever you are that will love our river and meadow, be gentle in your mind toward the Place, as we were. Observe with love and understanding and you will reap rich rewards.

You will observe what we observed, for the Place will not change, unless it is crowded out by people and houses. There will be a hawk over the meadow, there will be wild things and flowers and trees. There will be the river and the pond; the songs of the frogs. The things we have loved will be the same.

We will change. No, we have changed. I see Steven moving ahead of me down the river path. Looking at that tall figure and those broad shoulders, I remember a slighter figure. He has a job now and a car and will soon go to college. We talk at the campfire about yearbooks and career planning and rock groups. It has been a while since we dusted off our little plastic men and their horses and weapons.

This is as it should be. We can live only so long in the Secret Place, where animals talk and play games. Then we must store that world in our memories, although we will bring it out once in a while, like our little plastic people.

As long as we have those memories, the world of reality is much easier to live in and this is why this book was written—to share memories.

The other day we were walking along the river path toward the campsite. Steven stopped and very slowly raised the binoculars. For long moments he stared, fascinated. It was no rare happening, no unusual bird or wild thing. It was only a woodpecker, busily hammering the branch of an old dead tree.

We can find wonder in the ordinary as well as the exotic. The world of the ant is as meaningful as the world of the eagle: neither is favored in the plan. My wish is that Steven will never cease to wonder at the importance and the beauty of all worlds.

Today is Thursday.

Tomorrow night we will build our fire at the campsite.

The wild things will be there and we will feel the magic of the Secret Place.